THE LONELY PLANET
BOOK OF EVERYTHING
A Visual Guide to Travel and the World

NIGEL HOLMES

To Erin, with love to the
best travel partner anyone could
possibly wish for.

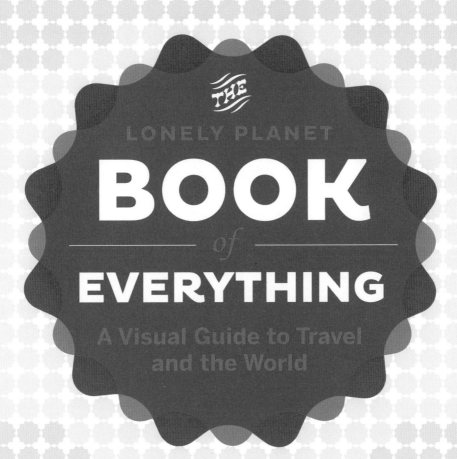

THE

LONELY PLANET

BOOK

of

EVERYTHING

A Visual Guide to Travel
and the World

NIGEL HOLMES

THE CONTENTS

CONTENTS

FOOD & DRINK
PAGE 118

PERSONAL SAFETY
PAGE 144

OTHER FUN STUFF
PAGE 156

Q.

QUICK QUESTION

The Book of EVERYTHING? How can that be?

A.

QUICK ANSWER

It can't be!

WE DID CONSIDER
OTHER TITLES

THE BOOK OF ALMOST EVERYTHING

**THE BOOK OF THINGS WE THOUGHT TRAVELLERS
MIGHT FIND INTERESTING**

**A WHOLE LOT OF FASCINATING
TRAVEL TRIVIA**

**HOW TO PLAY CROQUET, EAT BUGS IN THE JUNGLE,
DELIVER A BABY, SAY CHEERS
IN CHINESE AND ABOUT 78 OTHER THINGS**

...and so on, but none of them seemed quite right.

So *The Book of Everything* it is.

FOREWORD

PLEASE DON'T CONTACT US WITH COMPLAINTS SUCH AS

"I went on vacation to Belize in June, and it rained
hard every day. My husband wants to know why that
isn't in *The Book of Everything*."
Also, we should tell you right now that there's
nothing about packing your suitcase or backpack,
or prospecting for gold in Brazil, or surviving in the Antarctic,
or climbing Mount Everest, or dancing at Carnevale,
or anything at all about Mombasa, Mumbai or Montevideo,
or about tattooing, or about those flaps on an
aircraft's wings and what they do.
(Although we could explain that last one;
it's just not very interesting.)

Anyway, if you are looking for any of that information,
and have read this far but haven't bought the book yet,
then don't buy it—it's not right for you.

But everything else is within these pages,
so read on. It'll be fun. You'll see.

NIGEL HOLMES, JULY 2012

UNDERSTANDING THE WORLD

A different world

What's a travel book without a map of the world? And why
do we always look at it the same way? This view might help you
to see countries in a new light. (Then again it might just be totally annoying.)

New
Zealand

*It's great
to be at the top
for a change!*

Australia

Pacific
Islands

Papua
New
Guinea

Singapore

I n d o n e s i a

Malaysia

Brunei

Philippines

Vietnam

Hong Kong

Taiwan

Japan

S. Korea

N. Korea

Laos

Myanmar

Cambodia

Thailand

Bangladesh

India

Sri Lanka

Nepal

Bhutan

China

Tajikistan

Mongolia

Kazakhstan

Russia

Pakistan

Afghanistan

Turkmenistan

Uzbekistan

Azerbaijan

Armenia

Iran

Iraq

UAE

Saudi
Arabia

Kuwait

Syria

Cyprus

Turkey

Israel

*Some
smaller countries
haven't been named.*

Mauritius

Tanzania

Madagascar

Djibouti
Eritrea

Somalia

Palestine

Jordan

Bahrain

Oman

Lebanon

Yemen

Ethiopia

Burundi
Rwanda
Uganda

Kenya

Lesotho

Swaziland

Mozambique

Malawi

South Africa

Namibia

Zimbabwe

Botswana

Zambia

Angola

Dem. Rep.
of Congo

Congo

Gabon

Equatorial Guinea

Ivory Coast

Benin

Togo

Liberia

Sierra Leone

Guinea-
Bissau

Gambia

Senegal

South
Sudan

Central
African
Republic

Cameroon

Ghana

Nigeria

Burkina
Faso

Guinea

Sudan

Chad

Niger

Mali

Mauritania

Western
Sahara

Egypt

Libya

Algeria

Morocco

Macedonia

Tunisia

Greece

Albania

Italy

Spain

Portugal

Bulgaria

Serbia

Romania

Croatia

France

Switzerland

Moldova

Austria

Ukraine

Germany

Ireland

Belarus

Poland

United Kingdom

Lithuania

Denmark

Latvia

Estonia

Belgium

Netherlands

Norway

Finland

Sweden

Iceland

Czech Republic

Slovakia

Hungary

Is it really upside down?

Our custom of orienting maps with north at the top is arbitrary. The Greek cartographer and astronomer Ptolemy drew his maps that way around the year AD 150, and most mapmakers have followed his example.

Some people think that north-oriented maps have an implicit bias toward the northern hemisphere, and many classic (and still used) world projections do favour the northern hemisphere. This is because at the time these maps were made, most of the developed world was in the north and more room was needed to show the detail in this area.

When the famous photo of Earth taken from space (aboard Apollo 17) was first published, in 1972, it showed the South Pole like this:

That's Africa, or rather, Africa.

NASA

Publications quickly turned the image round to fit the established convention.

Uruguay

Chile

Argentina

Paraguay

Bolivia

Peru

Brazil

Guyana

Ecuador

French Guiana

Colombia

Costa Rica

Suriname

Panama

Venezuela

Nicaragua

El Salvador

Jamaica

Haiti

Guatemala

Caribbean Islands

Puerto Rico

Honduras

Dominican Rep.

Cuba

Belize

Bahamas

Mexico

Bermuda

Hawaii →

United States

Canada

Greenland

Around the world: the equator

The first person to sail around the globe was Juan Sebastián del Cano, who took credit after his captain, Ferdinand Magellan, was killed en route. The voyage lasted almost 3 years, from 1519 to 1522.

In 1961, Russian cosmonaut Yuri Gagarin was the first to make the trip into space. It took 1 hour and 48 minutes.

You can set foot on only about 8,000km (5,000 miles; 20%) of the Equator's length, **in the places shown in red.**

The Pacific Ocean alone accounts for 18,000km (about 11,000 miles) of water around the middle of the Earth.

EQUATOR

P A C I F I C   O C E A N

ATLANTIC OCEAN

INDIAN OCEAN

Galápagos Islands

Ecuador

Colombia

Brazil

Malaku (Moluccas)
Sulawesi (Celebes)

Borneo

Sumatra

Maldives

Dem. Republic of Congo

Gabon
Congo
Uganda
Kenya
Somalia

Equator days are the same year round: 12 hours of daylight, 12 of darkness. The sun rises around 6am and sets around 6pm.

Global climate change has special urgency in the **Maldives.** If the sea level continues rising at current rates, most of the 1,200 islands and atolls will be under water by 2100, according to the UN.

Time it takes light to travel around the equator: **0.13 of a second.**

Time it would take a baseball travelling at 160km/h (100mph): **10 days.**

Time it would take running nonstop at 10.5km/h (6.5mph): **160 days.**

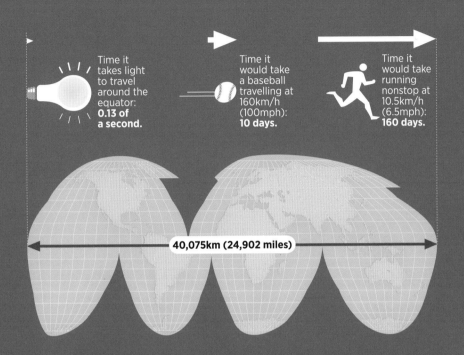

40,075km (24,902 miles)

Why it's so darn hot

It's hot almost everywhere on the equator because the sun's rays hit the earth there straight on, heating the ground and the air above it. Elsewhere, the rays hit the atmosphere at an angle because the earth is curved. This dissipates some of the sun's energy.

Arctic
Sun's rays are almost horizontal

Equator
Sun's rays are directly overhead

Elsewhere
Sun's rays are angled

Antarctic
Sun's rays are almost horizontal

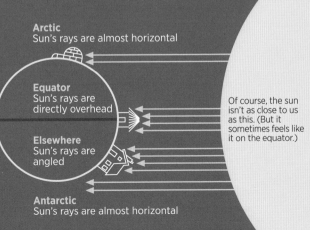

Of course, the sun isn't as close to us as this. (But it sometimes feels like it on the equator.)

13

The world's highest mountains

The really high ones are all in Asia. Shown here 👉 are Asia's top five.

(There are 60 other peaks in Asia that are higher than the tallest in South America, below.)

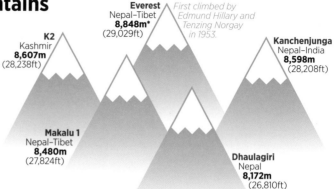

The top of **Asia**

Everest
Nepal-Tibet
8,848m*
(29,029ft)

First climbed by Edmund Hillary and Tenzing Norgay in 1953.

K2
Kashmir
8,607m
(28,238ft)

Kanchenjunga
Nepal-India
8,598m
(28,208ft)

Makalu 1
Nepal-Tibet
8,480m
(27,824ft)

Dhaulagiri
Nepal
8,172m
(26,810ft)

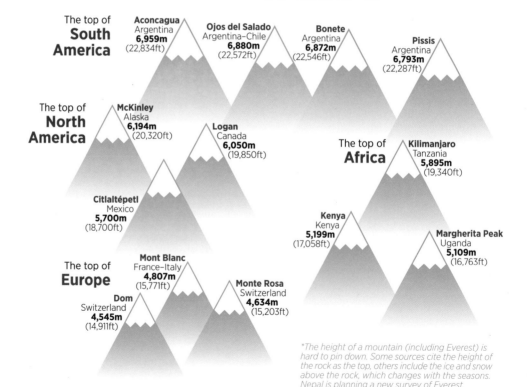

The top of **South America**

Aconcagua
Argentina
6,959m
(22,834ft)

Ojos del Salado
Argentina–Chile
6,880m
(22,572ft)

Bonete
Argentina
6,872m
(22,546ft)

Pissis
Argentina
6,793m
(22,287ft)

The top of **North America**

McKinley
Alaska
6,194m
(20,320ft)

Logan
Canada
6,050m
(19,850ft)

Citlaltépetl
Mexico
5,700m
(18,700ft)

The top of **Africa**

Kilimanjaro
Tanzania
5,895m
(19,340ft)

Kenya
Kenya
5,199m
(17,058ft)

Margherita Peak
Uganda
5,109m
(16,763ft)

The top of **Europe**

Mont Blanc
France–Italy
4,807m
(15,771ft)

Monte Rosa
Switzerland
4,634m
(15,203ft)

Dom
Switzerland
4,545m
(14,911ft)

The height of a mountain (including Everest) is hard to pin down. Some sources cite the height of the rock as the top, others include the ice and snow above the rock, which changes with the seasons. Nepal is planning a new survey of Everest.

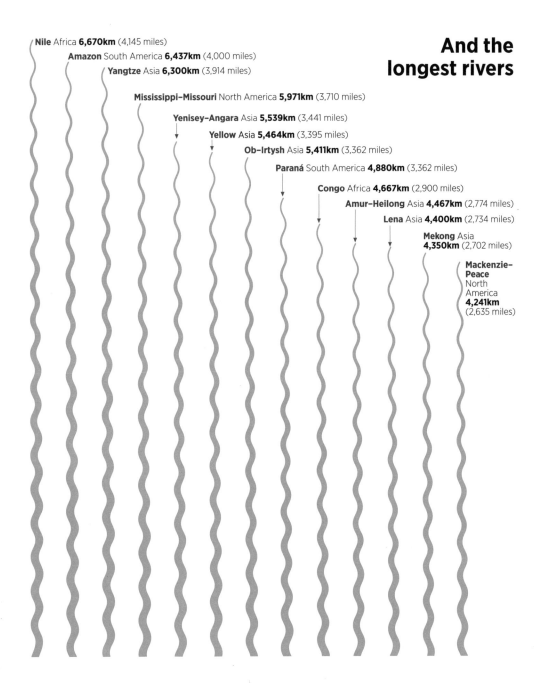

Nile Africa **6,670km** (4,145 miles)

Amazon South America **6,437km** (4,000 miles)

Yangtze Asia **6,300km** (3,914 miles)

Mississippi–Missouri North America **5,971km** (3,710 miles)

Yenisey–Angara Asia **5,539km** (3,441 miles)

Yellow Asia **5,464km** (3,395 miles)

Ob–Irtysh Asia **5,411km** (3,362 miles)

Paraná South America **4,880km** (3,362 miles)

Congo Africa **4,667km** (2,900 miles)

Amur–Heilong Asia **4,467km** (2,774 miles)

Lena Asia **4,400km** (2,734 miles)

Mekong Asia **4,350km** (2,702 miles)

Mackenzie–Peace North America **4,241km** (2,635 miles)

And the longest rivers

What are the "Northern Lights"?

Properly known as the **Aurora Borealis,** they are a wonderful sight that lights up the northern night sky. (Aurora was the Roman goddess of dawn; Boreas is the Greek name for the north wind.) Here's the science behind what you see.

1

Streams of charged particles (electrons and protons) flow from the sun to Earth at a velocity of over 1.4 million km/h (900 thousand mph).

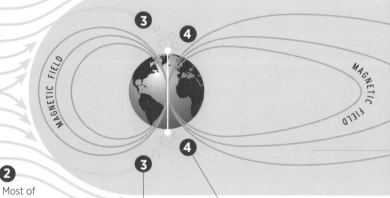

2

Most of the particles are deflected by Earth's magnetosphere, (shown here in light blue …)

3 but some are sucked into the vortex of Earth's magnetic fields (pink lines) at the North and South Poles. (In the south, the effect is called **Aurora Australis,** or the Southern Lights.)

4 What we see as an aurora is the interaction of those charged particles with atoms from Earth's atmosphere. They form an oval ring around each pole.

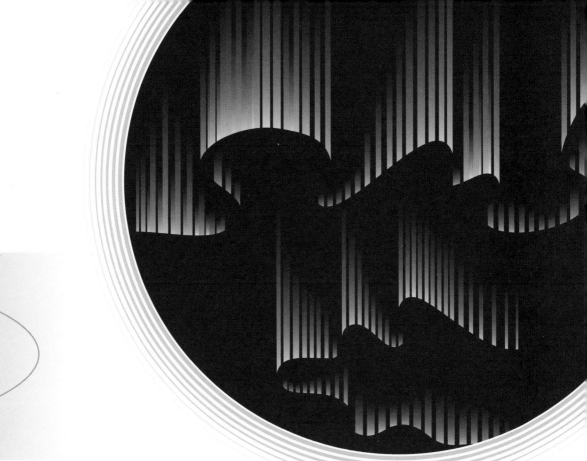

Shown here is one type of aurora, which appears like billowing curtains hanging in the air. (The other common effect is a diffuse glow swirling across the sky.) Auroras vary in colour from fluorescent greens to soft reds and yellows.

Where (and when) are the best places to view the "lights"?
Wherever you are, you need a clear, dark sky.
The best time is around midnight in winter.

To see the Aurora Borealis in the **north,** go to Alaska, Canada, Greenland, Scandinavia and the northern coast of Siberia. Wear warm clothes.

To see the Aurora Australis in the **south,** your best bets are Antarctica, South America, Tasmania and the southern tip of New Zealand.

What do those signs mean?

How to read the signals that the guy on the runway is giving to your pilot.
(They're called marshalling signals.)

start engines

move ahead

turn to your left

turn to your right

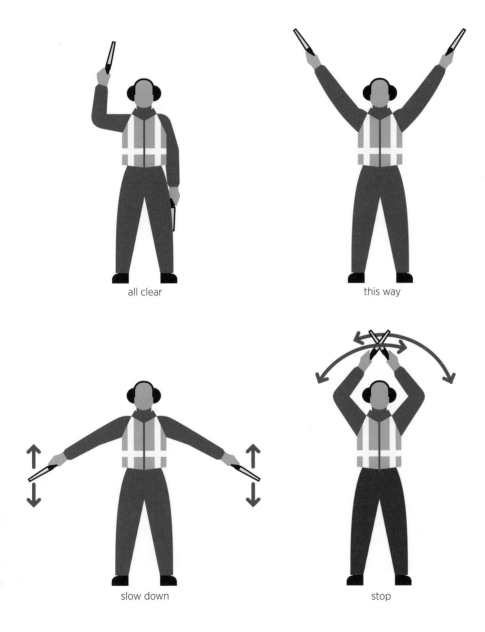

all clear

this way

slow down

stop

The world's most commonly spoken languages

The total number of **countries** using these languages.*

●●●●●●●

English ●●●
480 million speakers (the number of native speakers, plus those for whom it is a second language)

French ●●●●●●●●●●●●●●●●●●●●●●●●●●●●●●●●●●● **35** countries
265 million speakers

Arabic ●●●●●●●●●●●●●●●●●●●●●●● **24** countries
221 million speakers

Spanish ●●●●●●●●●●●●●●●●●●● **20** countries
320 million speakers

Russian ●●●●●●●●●●●●●●● **16** countries
285 million speakers

German ●●●●●●●● **9** countries
109 million speakers

Mandarin ●●●●● **5** countries
1.1 billion speakers

Portuguese ●●●●● **5** countries
188 million speakers

Hindi/Urdu ●● **2** countries
250 million speakers

Bengali ● **1** country
185 million speakers

Japanese ● **1** country
133 million speakers

If you go to a country where you don't know a word of the language, *Google Translate* can help. It has 63 languages, and is available as a free app on iPhone and Android smartphones.

*The number of countries includes those where the language has full legal or official status and where it is an influential minority language (such as English in India).

In addition, the list includes countries where the language is used in trade or tourism, or is the preferred language of the young (such as English in Japan).

Linguists say that the world's most difficult language is spoken in Botswana. It includes 75 different mouth clicks along with regular words.

	0	1	2	3	4
Arabic	sifr	wahid	'itnan	talata	'arba'a
Basque	zero	bat	bi	hiru	lau
Cheyenne		na'estse	nese	na'he	neve
Danish	nul	en	to	tre	fire
Dutch	nul	een	twee	drie	vier
Esperanto	nul	unu	du	tri	kvar
French	zéro	un	deux	trois	quatre
Fijian	saiva	dua	rua	tolu	vaa
German	null	eins	zwei	drei	vier
Hindi		ek	do	teen	char
Hungarian	nulla	egy	ketto	harom	negy
Italian	zero	uno	due	tre	quattro
Japanese		ichi	ni	san	shi/yon
Korean		il	i	sam	sa
Mandarin	ling	yi	er/liang	san	si
Norwegian	null	en	to	tre	fire
Persian	sefr	yek	do	se	charhar
Polish	zero	jeden	dwa	trzy	cztery
Portuguese	zero	um	dois	tres	quatro
Russian	nol	odin	dva	tri	cetyre
Spanish	cero	uno	dos	tres	cuatro
Swahili	sifuri	moja	mbili	tatu	nne
Swedish	noll	en	tva	tre	fyra
Turkish	sifir	bir	iki	üç	dört
Zulu	iqanda	kunye	kubili	kuthathu	kune

5	6	7	8	9	10
hamsa	sitta	sab'a	tamaniya	tis'a	'asara
bost	sei	zazpi	zortzi	bederatzi	hamar
noho	naesohto	nesohto	na'nohto	soohto	mahtohto
fem	seks	syv	otte	ni	ti
vijf	zes	zeven	acht	negen	tien
kvir	ses	sep	ok	nau	dek
cinq	six	sept	huit	neuf	dix
lima	ono	vitu	walu	ciwa	tini
funf	sechs	sieben	acht	neun	zehn
panch	che	saath	aath	noh	dus
ot	hat	het	nyolc	kilenc	tiz
cinque	sei	sette	otto	nove	dieci
go	roku	nana/shichi	hachi	ku/kyuu	jyuu
o	yuk	chil	pal	ku	sip
wu	liu	qi	ba	jiu	shi
fem	seks	sju	atte	ni	ti
panj	shesh	haft	hasht	noh	dah
piec	szesc	siedem	osiem	dziewiec	dziesiec
cinco	seis	sete	oito	nove	dez
pjat	sest	sem	vosem	devjat	desjat
cinco	seis	siete	ocho	nueve	diez
tano	sita	saba	nane	tisa	kumi
fem	sex	sju	atta	nio	tio
bes	alti	yedi	sekiz	dokuz	on
ishianu	isithuptha	isikhombisa	isishiya-galombili	isishiya galolunye	ishumi

Can't find the word?

Point!

Mother!

A look at one branch of the **world's language tree,** and how to say "hello" to a particularly important person.

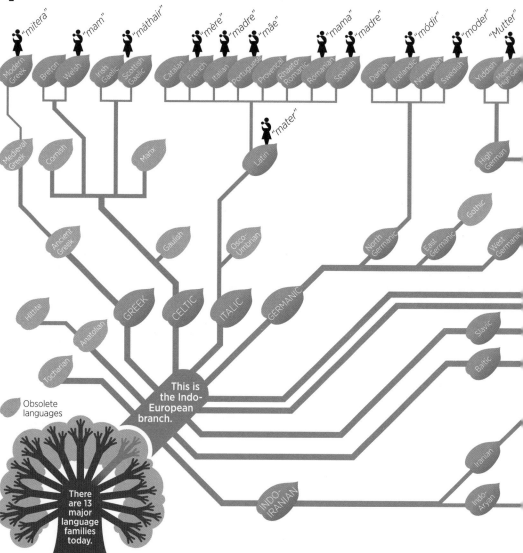

"mitera" — Modern Greek

"mam" — Breton · Welsh

"máthair" — Irish Gaelic · Scottish Gaelic

"mère" — French

"madre" — Catalan · Italian · Spanish

"mãe" — Portuguese

"mama" — Provençal · Rhaeto-Romanic · Romanian

"madre" — Spanish

"móðir" — Icelandic

"moder" — Danish · Norwegian · Swedish

"Mutter" — Yiddish · Modern High German

"mater" — Latin

Medieval Greek · Cornish · Manx · Ancient Greek · Gaulish · Osco-Umbrian · High German

North Germanic · East Germanic · Gothic · West Germanic

Hittite · Anatolian · GREEK · CELTIC · ITALIC · GERMANIC · Slavic · Baltic

Tocharian

Obsolete languages

This is the Indo-European branch.

There are 13 major language families today.

INDO-IRANIAN · Indo-Aryan · Iranian

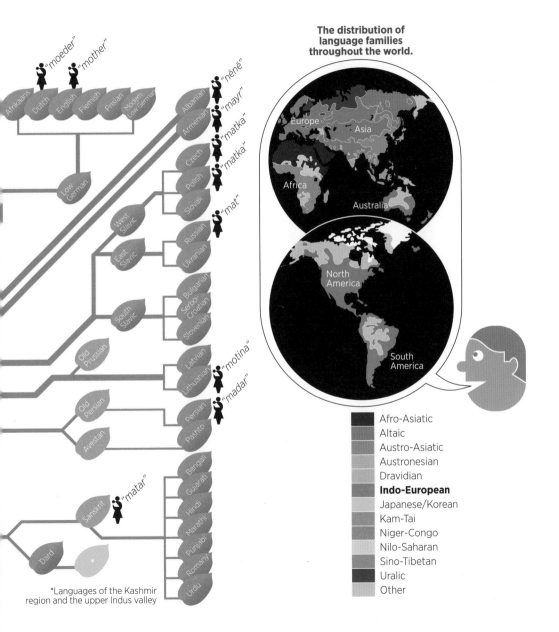

The distribution of
language families
throughout the world.

"moeder"   "mother"

Afrikaans Dutch English Flemish Frisian Modern Low German

Low German

Albanian

"nënë"

Armenian

"mayr"

Czech

"matka"

Polish

Slovak

"matka"

West Slavic

East Slavic

Russian

"mat"

Ukranian

South Slavic

Bulgarian

Serbo-Croatian

Slovenian

Old Prussian

Latvian

"motina"

Lithuanian

"madar"

Old Persian

Persian

Avestan

Pashto

Bengali

Gujarati

"matar"

Sanskrit

Hindi

Marathi

Dard

Punjabi

Romany

Urdu

Europe

Asia

Africa

Australia

North America

South America

Afro-Asiatic
Altaic
Austro-Asiatic
Austronesian
Dravidian
Indo-European
Japanese/Korean
Kam-Tai
Niger-Congo
Nilo-Saharan
Sino-Tibetan
Uralic
Other

*Languages of the Kashmir region and the upper Indus valley

How to read Egyptian hieroglyphs

(Greek for "sacred carvings")

It's more complicated than you think. This ancient writing system contains more than **2,000 symbols,** some more representational than others. Originating somewhere between 3100 BC and AD 40, the hieroglyphs were not understood until the 1799 discovery of the **Rosetta Stone** by soldiers in Napoleon's army in the town of Rosetta, Egypt.

The tabletop-sized slab of black rock was covered with texts in three languages: **Egyptian hieroglyphs, Greek and a second Egyptian script.** In 1822, a French language scholar, Jean-François Champollion, finally solved the riddle of the Stone, largely by matching up the pictorial Egyptian hieroglyphs with the readable Greek text.

You can see the Rosetta Stone in the British Museum, in London.

The structure of the language is complex—the signs are divided into three categories: one category for words, one for sounds and one that explains the meaning of the group of signs immediately preceding them— but we can still have fun by doing a simple form of Egyptian writing (try your own name, perhaps) using this **basic hieroglyphic alphabet.** 👉

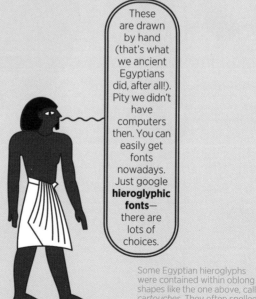

These are drawn by hand (that's what we ancient Egyptians did, after all!). Pity we didn't have computers then. You can easily get fonts nowadays. Just google **hieroglyphic fonts**— there are lots of choices.

Some Egyptian hieroglyphs were contained within oblong shapes like the one above, called *cartouches.* They often spelled out the names of Egypt's rulers.

A Vulture

B Foot
(Some say this also stands for V.)

C Basket

D Hand

E Flowering reed

F Horned viper

G Jar stand

H House (floor plan)

I Flowering reed

J Cobra

K Basket

L Lion

M Owl

N Water

O Lasso

P Seat

Q Hill

R Mouth

S Folded cloth

T Egyptian bread loaf

U, W Quail chick

X Basket and cloth

Y Two flowering reeds

Z Door bolt

Who's happy, who's not?

In April 2012, the Earth Institute at Columbia University in New York produced this ranking of countries for the UN Conference on Happiness. Since this is *The Book of **Everything***, here's the **whole list,** from happiest at the left to least happy down there ☞

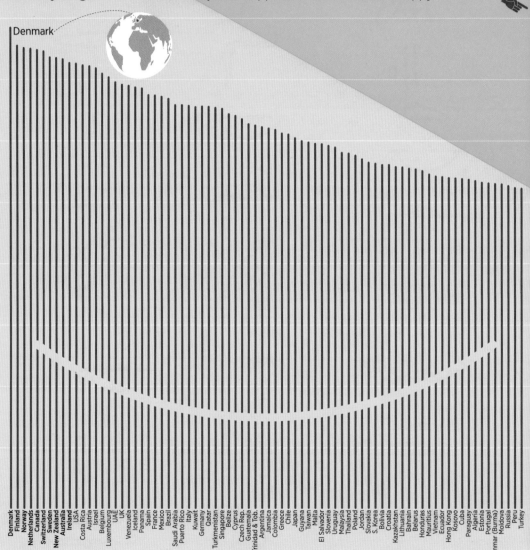

Denmark

Denmark
Finland
Norway
Netherlands
Canada
Switzerland
Sweden
New Zealand
Australia
Ireland
USA
Costa Rica
Austria
Israel
Belgium
Luxembourg
UAE
UK
Venezuela
Iceland
Panama
Spain
France
Mexico
Brazil
Saudi Arabia
Puerto Rico
Italy
Kuwait
Germany
Qatar
Turkmenistan
Singapore
Belize
Cyprus
Czech Rep.
Guatemala
Trinidad & Tob.
Argentina
Jamaica
Colombia
Greece
Chile
Japan
Guyana
Taiwan
Malta
El Salvador
Slovenia
Uruguay
Malaysia
Thailand
Poland
Jordan
Slovakia
S. Korea
Bolivia
Croatia
Kazakhstan
Lithuania
Bahrain
Belarus
Honduras
Mauritius
Vietnam
Ecuador
Hong Kong
Kosovo
Cuba
Paraguay
Algeria
Estonia
Portugal
Myanmar (Burma)
Moldova
Russia
Peru
Turkey

The list was compiled by averaging a number of factors, each scored from 0–10, in a kind of life-evaluation score. Factors included **government corruption, political freedom, physical and mental health, job security and family life.** So unlike previous, similar happiness lists, these rankings are not connected solely to **income.**

There are **156 countries** here. By most accounts, there are 196 countries in the world. The US does not recognise Taiwan as a separate country, and other places such as Bermuda, Greenland, Puerto Rico and Western Sahara are commonly mistaken to be independent.

Bhutan's Gross National Happiness (GNH) index, formalised in 2010, aims at the goal of happiness over the goal of wealth. But this was not a new thing for that country. The Bhutanese legal code of 1729 stated: **"If the Government cannot create happiness for its people, there is no purpose for the Government to exist."** Nice!

(While Bhutan is an inspiration for the current interest in happiness, it is not on the chart shown here, because it has not yet been included in the Gallup World Poll that was used as a source for the list.)

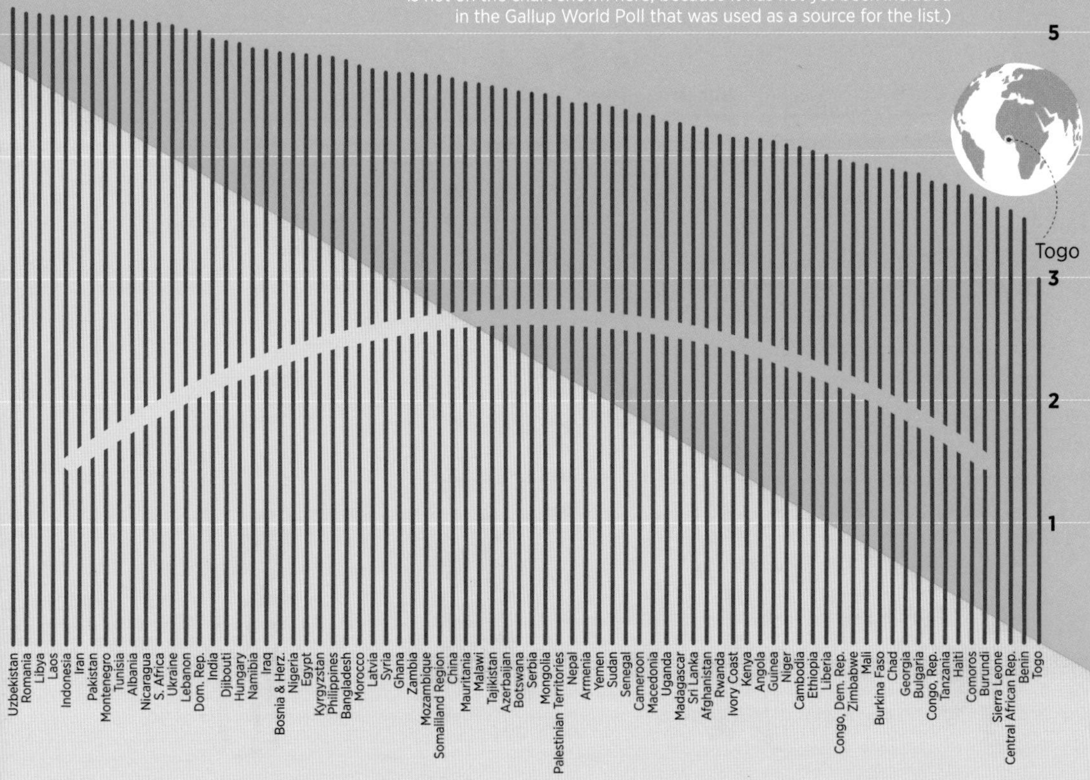

8

7

6

5

Togo

3

2

1

Uzbekistan
Romania
Libya
Laos
Indonesia
Iran
Pakistan
Montenegro
Tunisia
Albania
Nicaragua
Africa
Ukraine
Lebanon
Dom. Rep.
India
Djibouti
Hungary
Namibia
Iraq
Nigeria
Bosnia & Herz.
Egypt
Kyrgyzstan
Philippines
Bangladesh
Morocco
Latvia
Syria
Ghana
Zambia
Mozambique
Somaliland Region
China
Mauritania
Malawi
Tajikistan
Azerbaijan
Botswana
Serbia
Mongolia
Palestinian Territories
Nepal
Armenia
Yemen
Sudan
Senegal
Cameroon
Macedonia
Uganda
Madagascar
Sri Lanka
Afghanistan
Rwanda
Ivory Coast
Kenya
Angola
Guinea
Niger
Cambodia
Ethiopia
Liberia
Congo, Dem. Rep.
Zimbabwe
Mali
Burkina Faso
Chad
Georgia
Bulgaria
Congo, Rep.
Tanzania
Haiti
Comoros
Burundi
Sierra Leone
Central African Rep.
Benin
Togo

UNDERSTANDING THE WORLD

Disappearing diversity

There are over 5,000 indigenous groups in the world. They represent many ways that humans have adapted to almost every environment.

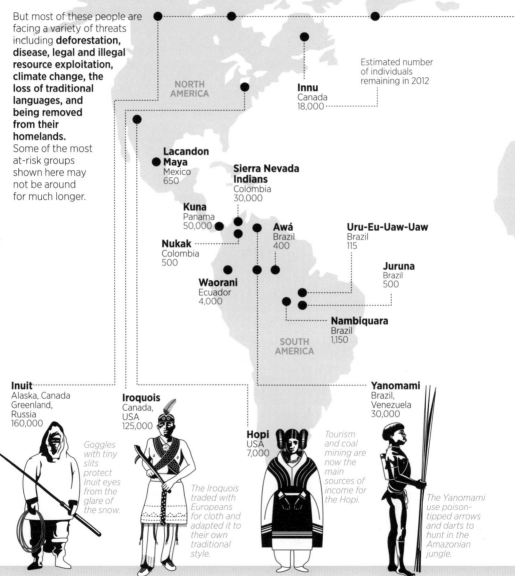

But most of these people are facing a variety of threats including **deforestation, disease, legal and illegal resource exploitation, climate change, the loss of traditional languages, and being removed from their homelands.** Some of the most at-risk groups shown here may not be around for much longer.

NORTH
AMERICA

Estimated number
of individuals
remaining in 2012

Innu
Canada
18,000

**Lacandon
Maya**
Mexico
650

**Sierra Nevada
Indians**
Colombia
30,000

Kuna
Panama
50,000

Awá
Brazil
400

Uru-Eu-Uaw-Uaw
Brazil
115

Nukak
Colombia
500

Juruna
Brazil
500

Waorani
Ecuador
4,000

Nambiquara
Brazil
1,150

SOUTH
AMERICA

Inuit
Alaska, Canada
Greenland,
Russia
160,000

Iroquois
Canada,
USA
125,000

*Goggles
with tiny
slits
protect
Inuit eyes
from the
glare of
the snow.*

*The Iroquois
traded with
Europeans
for cloth and
adapted it to
their own
traditional
style.*

Hopi
USA
7,000

*Tourism
and coal
mining are
now the
main
sources of
income for
the Hopi.*

Yanomami
Brazil,
Venezuela
30,000

*The Yanomami
use poison-
tipped arrows
and darts to
hunt in the
Amazonian
jungle.*

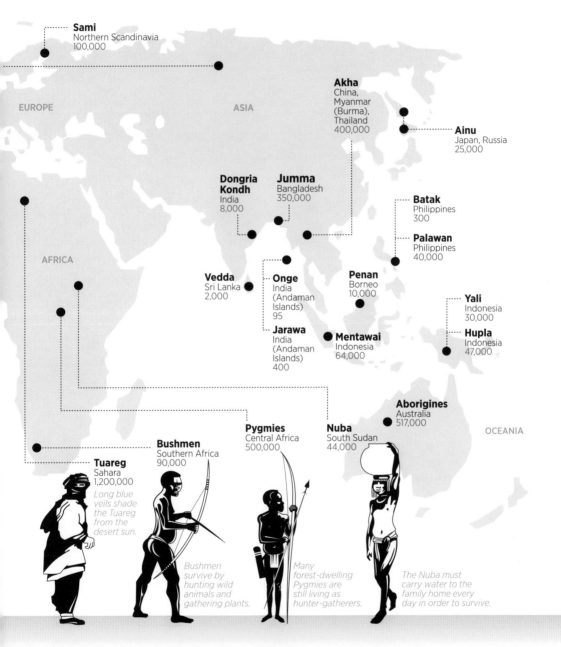

Sami
Northern Scandinavia
100,000

Akha
China,
Myanmar
(Burma),
Thailand
400,000

Ainu
Japan, Russia
25,000

Dongria Kondh
India
8,000

Jumma
Bangladesh
350,000

Batak
Philippines
300

Palawan
Philippines
40,000

Vedda
Sri Lanka
2,000

Onge
India
(Andaman
Islands)
95

Penan
Borneo
10,000

Yali
Indonesia
30,000

Jarawa
India
(Andaman
Islands)
400

Mentawai
Indonesia
64,000

Hupla
Indonesia
47,000

Aborigines
Australia
517,000

EUROPE

ASIA

AFRICA

OCEANIA

Tuareg
Sahara
1,200,000
Long blue veils shade the Tuareg from the desert sun.

Bushmen
Southern Africa
90,000
Bushmen survive by hunting wild animals and gathering plants.

Pygmies
Central Africa
500,000
Many forest-dwelling Pygmies are still living as hunter-gatherers.

Nuba
South Sudan
44,000
The Nuba must carry water to the family home every day in order to survive.

How to predict the weather from the clouds

Long before the digital "cloud", there was the weather forecasting cloud. But do we ever believe the weather forecast? That science is more complicated than just looking at the clouds, of course, but this guide might just help you plan that picnic next weekend.

metres
12,200

What the names mean
Cirrus Curl (as of hair)
Stratus Layer, spread over an area
Cumulus Heap of clouds
Nimbus Rain-bearing

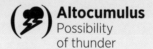
Cirrostratus
Rain in the next
12–24 hours

9,150

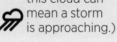
Cirrocumulus
Fair weather
(In the tropics,
this cloud can
mean a storm
is approaching.)

Altocumulus
Possibility
of thunder

7,000

Nimbostratus
Rain

3,050

Stratus
(This cloud looks
like elevated fog.)
Drizzle,
light snow

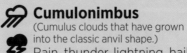

Cumulonimbus
(Cumulus clouds that have grown into the classic anvil shape.)
Rain, thunder, lightning, hail, flash floods, tornadoes

feet
40,000

 **Cirrus**
Fair weather

30,000   Cruising altitude of jet airliners

The phrase "cloud nine" is said to have originated with the US Weather Bureau, which once classified clouds by number. Cumulonimbus was number nine on the list, since it's the cloud that climbs farthest into the sky. So if you're on cloud nine, you're happily on top of the world.*

 **Altostratus**
Rain in the next
12–24 hours

20,000

*A little scepticism is in order.
1. There are generally considered to be **ten** distinct cloud formations.
2. This might be the tallest cloud, but it's not the happiest!

Cumulus
Fair weather

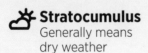 **Stratocumulus**
Generally means
dry weather

10,000

35

Snow?
What's that?

Most scientists agree that global climate change is real. That could mean that in a few years (well, quite a few years in the future) these two pages might describe a quaint and forgotten weather effect. In the meantime, find some snow and go skiing.

Here's how snow starts and then changes on its way down.

1 Between 11 and 13 kilometres (7–8 miles) above the earth, water vapour condenses and becomes liquid.

2 The droplets grow and form ice crystals around minute particles floating in the atmosphere.

Pollen or dust particle

Look at all these Eskimo words for snow!*

MAUJA
(deep, soft snow)

UPSIK
(compacted snow)

APUN
(snow on the ground)

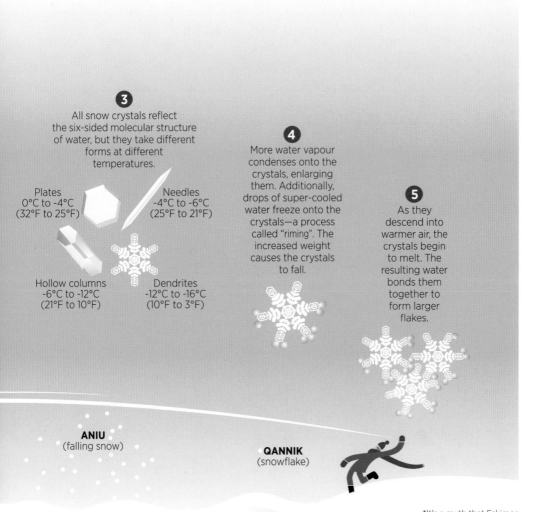

3

All snow crystals reflect the six-sided molecular structure of water, but they take different forms at different temperatures.

Plates
0°C to -4°C
(32°F to 25°F)

Needles
-4°C to -6°C
(25°F to 21°F)

Hollow columns
-6°C to -12°C
(21°F to 10°F)

Dendrites
-12°C to -16°C
(10°F to 3°F)

4

More water vapour condenses onto the crystals, enlarging them. Additionally, drops of super-cooled water freeze onto the crystals—a process called "riming". The increased weight causes the crystals to fall.

5

As they descend into warmer air, the crystals begin to melt. The resulting water bonds them together to form larger flakes.

ANIU
(falling snow)

QANNIK
(snowflake)

*It's a myth that Eskimos have hundreds of words for snow. The ones above are about it.

The **Sami**, however, *do* have very many names for the quality, depth and what-animal-has-just-been-on-it snow. The Sami are an Arctic indigenous people who live in the far north of Sweden, Norway, Finland and Russia.

The world's electrical outlets

Most countries use one or more of these 13 shapes.
(A selection of representative countries are listed.)
Make sure your appliances have the right plugs or adaptors.

Type A   **Type B**

Antigua, Bahamas,
Barbados, Belize,
Bermuda, Brazil, Canada,
China, Colombia, Costa
Rica, Ecuador,
Guatemala, Honduras,
Jamaica, Japan, Libya,
Mexico, Panama, Peru,
Puerto Rico, Saudi
Arabia, Tahiti, Thailand,
USA, Venezuela

Type C

Afghanistan, Albania, Algeria,
Angola, Argentina, Armenia,
Bolivia, Brazil, Bulgaria, Cambodia,
Canary Islands, Chile, Croatia,
Denmark, Egypt, Finland, Gabon,
Germany, Greece, Hungary,
Iceland, India, Indonesia, Iran, Iraq,
Israel, Italy, Macedonia,
Madagascar, Mongolia, Morocco,
Mozambique, Nepal, Netherlands,
Norway, Pakistan, Peru, Poland,
Portugal, Russia, Serbia, Somalia,
South Korea, Spain, Sudan,
Sweden, Syria, Thailand, Tunisia,
Turkey, Ukraine, Zambia

Type D

Ethiopia, Ghana,
Greece, India, Iraq,
Kuwait, Nepal,
Nigeria, Pakistan,
Sudan, Zambia,
Zimbabwe

Type H

Gaza,
Israel

Type I

Argentina,
Australia, China,
Fiji, Guatemala,
New Zealand,
Samoa

Type J

Ethiopia,
Switzerland

Type E

Belgium, Benin, Cambodia, Canary Islands, Czech Republic, France, Greece, Madagascar, Mongolia, Morocco, Poland, Slovak Republic, Syria, Tahiti, Tunisia

Type F

Afghanistan, Albania, Algeria, Austria, Bulgaria, Croatia, Finland, Germany, Greece, Hungary, Iceland, Indonesia, Italy, Macedonia, Mozambique, Netherlands, Norway, Portugal, Russia, Saudi Arabia, South Korea, Spain, Sweden, Turkey

Type G

Bahrain, Channel Islands, China, Cyprus, Ghana, Guatemala, Hong Kong, Indonesia, Iraq, Ireland, Kenya, Kuwait, Malawi, Malaysia, Malta, Nigeria, Saudi Arabia, Seychelles, Singapore, St Lucia, Uganda, UK, Zambia, Zimbabwe

Type K

Denmark

Type L

Canary Islands, Chile, Ethiopia, Italy, Syria

Type M

Botswana, Hong Kong, Mozambique, Namibia, South Africa

OUTDOOR SURVIVAL

Alligators and crocodiles: precautions ...

1 Sounds obvious, but **don't swim** (or dangle your arm off a boat) in lakes and rivers that locals warn you might have crocs or gators in them.

2 If you see one, **stay at least 4.5m (15ft) away.** In the water they can swim much faster than you; on land, they can move surprisingly quickly, so ...

3 On land, **run** in a straight line away from the water. They will pursue you moving very fast, but only for a short time, before tiring and giving up.

The tail provides the main thrust when swimming ...

and back claws are webbed to give extra propulsion in the water.

That's why they can swim faster than you. Don't try to find out if it's true!

and defensive measures

**OK, so you tried to get out of the way,
but one of them catches you. Here's what to do:**

(4) **Poke the eyes** with a stick, or anything you have.
Their eyes are their most vulnerable part.

(5) **Strike the nostrils and ears hard,**
with your fist or a heavy stick.

The ears (↓) are just behind the
eyes, hard to see. There are
movable flaps over them that
stop water from going in.

The nostrils are on top
of the snout so that the
rest of the body can be
submerged, out of sight.

(6) If your arm or leg is inside the mouth, you might
be able to **push the palatal valve down to the tongue.** ☞
Water will flow in, and the animal will let you go.

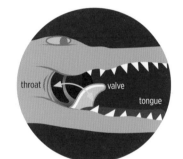

throat   valve   tongue

The palatal valve
is a flap of tissue
behind the tongue
that swings back
to close off the
throat and prevent
drowning when
the mouth is open.

Teeth are not used for
chewing; they grab
and hold prey—you!
(Although you're by no
means their main prey,
which is usually
swallowed whole.)

How to survive (and prevent) a shark attack

Keep your fears in proportion; you are more likely to be hurt by overexposure to the sun than you are to be bitten by a shark.

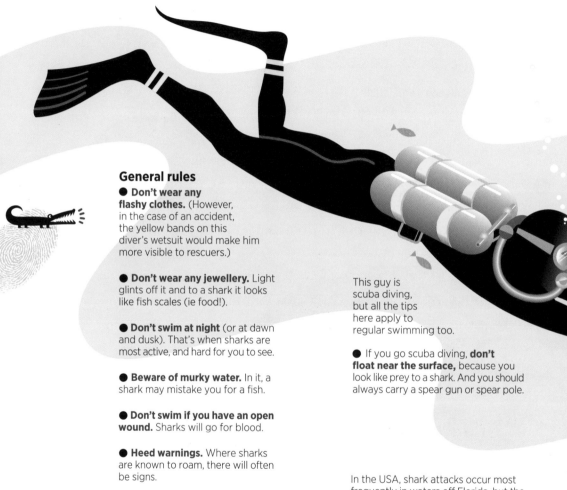

General rules

● **Don't wear any flashy clothes.** (However, in the case of an accident, the yellow bands on this diver's wetsuit would make him more visible to rescuers.)

● **Don't wear any jewellery.** Light glints off it and to a shark it looks like fish scales (ie food!).

● **Don't swim at night** (or at dawn and dusk). That's when sharks are most active, and hard for you to see.

● **Beware of murky water.** In it, a shark may mistake you for a fish.

● **Don't swim if you have an open wound.** Sharks will go for blood.

● **Heed warnings.** Where sharks are known to roam, there will often be signs.

● **Stay away from deep drop-offs underwater.** This is where sharks like to congregate.

This guy is scuba diving, but all the tips here apply to regular swimming too.

● If you go scuba diving, **don't float near the surface,** because you look like prey to a shark. And you should always carry a spear gun or spear pole.

In the USA, shark attacks occur most frequently in waters off Florida, but the California coast and all around Hawaii are also dangerous, as well as waters around Australia and South Africa.

Basic self-defence

● **Stay in groups while you swim.**
Sharks are less likely to attack
a group of swimmers than
an individual.

● **If a shark approaches you,** use
anything you have to strike at it—
your camera, for instance, or your
fist or a spear gun.

● **Don't go for the nose:**
a shark's eyes and gills are the most
sensitive and painful areas to hit.

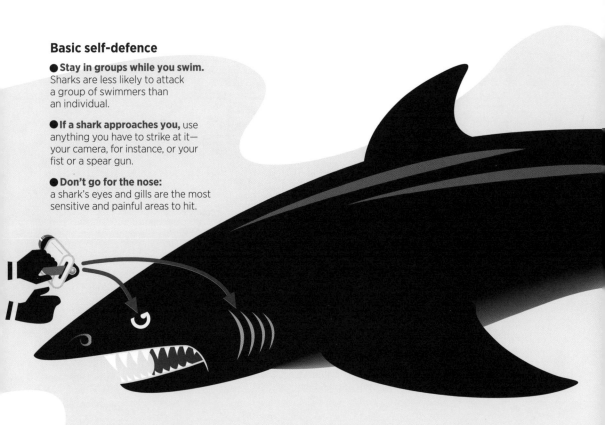

THE THREE MOST DANGEROUS SHARKS (average lengths)

GREAT WHITE 4.5m (15ft)   **TIGER** 3m (10ft)   **BULL** 2m (7ft)

How to avoid being sucked into quicksand ...

It's usually found near coasts and inland on riverbanks or near lakes, marshes and underground springs.

1 If you are walking in an area known to have quicksands, carry a **strong pole** with you.

2 If you feel yourself sinking, put the pole on the ground in front of you.

3 With the pole perpendicular to your body, lie across the pole.

4 Don't panic. The more you wiggle around, the faster you will sink. But **you will never sink completely,** because your body is not as dense as the surrounding sand. (You know you can float on water, and sand is denser than water; so it's easier to float in quicksand than on water.) **If you don't have a pole, don't worry, you'll still float.**

In general, quicksand is not that deep. The problem is the vacuum that's formed when you try to lift your legs once they are in the sand— jerky movements will suck you in further.

5 Spread your arms out to increase your surface area. Lie back and relax. With gentle movements, slowly work yourself to a safe area.

(I know, easier said than done!)

Quicksands are often depicted in movies as deadly: in real life they are not.

but if you can't, this is what's happening under you

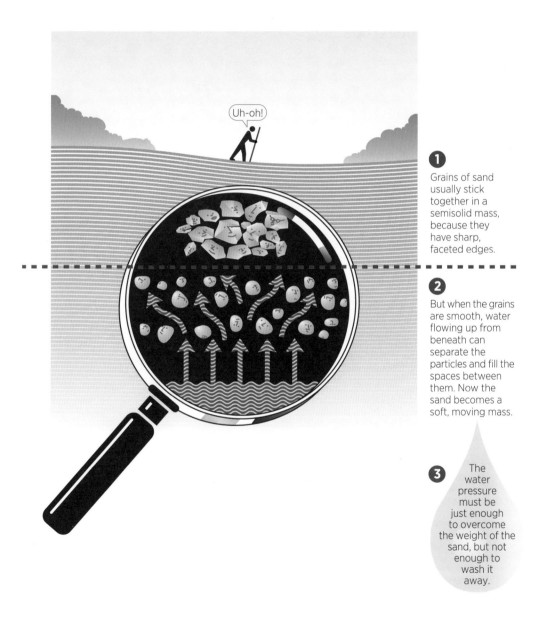

1 Grains of sand usually stick together in a semisolid mass, because they have sharp, faceted edges.

2 But when the grains are smooth, water flowing up from beneath can separate the particles and fill the spaces between them. Now the sand becomes a soft, moving mass.

3 The water pressure must be just enough to overcome the weight of the sand, but not enough to wash it away.

How to stop mosquitoes from fuelling up ... on you

(Spanish for "little fly")

THEY'LL DRINK YOUR BLOOD ...

Hidden inside the mosquito's proboscis are six "stylets" (hypodermic-like needles) that penetrate just far enough under the skin to find a blood vessel*.

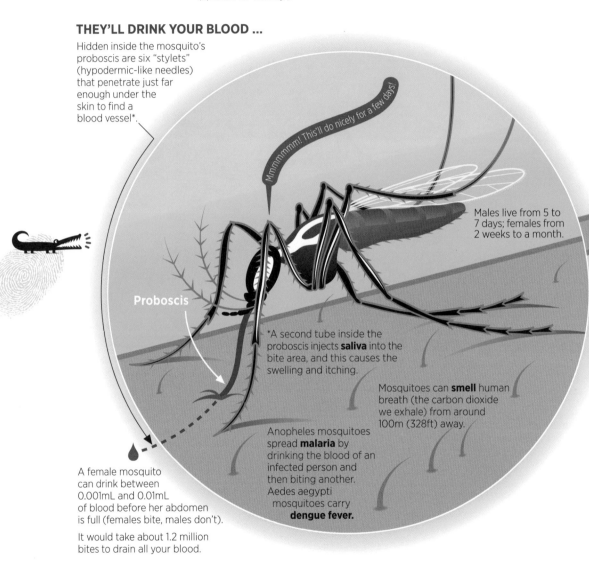

Mmmmmmm! This'll do nicely for a few days!

Males live from 5 to 7 days; females from 2 weeks to a month.

Proboscis

*A second tube inside the proboscis injects **saliva** into the bite area, and this causes the swelling and itching.

Mosquitoes can **smell** human breath (the carbon dioxide we exhale) from around 100m (328ft) away.

Anopheles mosquitoes spread **malaria** by drinking the blood of an infected person and then biting another. Aedes aegypti mosquitoes carry **dengue fever.**

A female mosquito can drink between 0.001mL and 0.01mL of blood before her abdomen is full (females bite, males don't).

It would take about 1.2 million bites to drain all your blood.

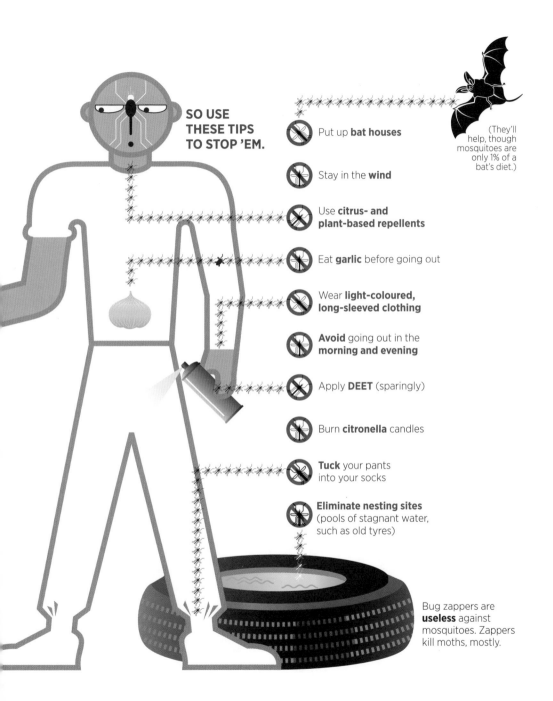

SO USE THESE TIPS TO STOP 'EM.

🚫 Put up **bat houses**

(They'll help, though mosquitoes are only 1% of a bat's diet.)

🚫 Stay in the **wind**

🚫 Use **citrus- and plant-based repellents**

🚫 Eat **garlic** before going out

🚫 Wear **light-coloured, long-sleeved clothing**

🚫 **Avoid** going out in the **morning and evening**

🚫 Apply **DEET** (sparingly)

🚫 Burn **citronella** candles

🚫 **Tuck** your pants into your socks

🚫 **Eliminate nesting sites** (pools of stagnant water, such as old tyres)

Bug zappers are **useless** against mosquitoes. Zappers kill moths, mostly.

Recognising animal tracks

See who's been walking around. Africa, this page,
and North America, opposite.

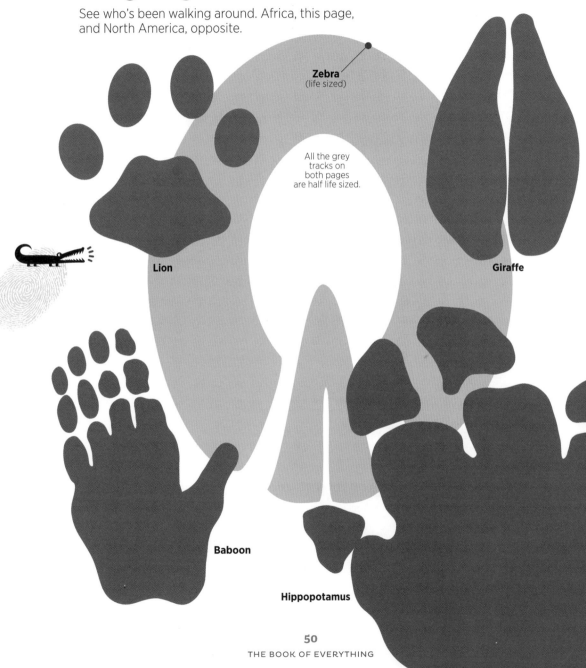

Zebra
(life sized)

All the grey
tracks on
both pages
are half life sized.

Lion

Giraffe

Baboon

Hippopotamus

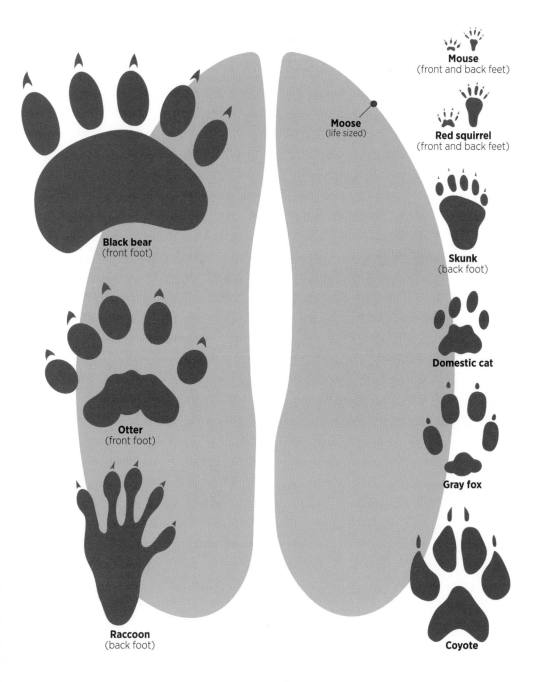

Mouse
(front and back feet)

Red squirrel
(front and back feet)

Moose
(life sized)

Skunk
(back foot)

Domestic cat

Gray fox

Black bear
(front foot)

Otter
(front foot)

Coyote

Raccoon
(back foot)

Recognising animal poop
Smart hikers call it **scat.** All these are drawn **life sized.**

Mouse Their scat is found near their nests, and can take lots of different irregular shapes.

Red squirrel This scat is very similar to that of the grey squirrel, but while red squirrels prefer a coniferous habitat, greys prefer a deciduous one, so where you find it is the best way to tell their poop apart.

Beaver The poop is composed of wood chips, but it's almost never seen because beavers spend most of their time in water, where the poop decomposes.

Weasel The scat is twisted into a long cylinder, and contains hair and bone splinters.

Porcupine You'll see bark, twigs and tree buds in porcupoop. It has a strong smell of urine. The scat may be found as separate pellets or in a chain linked by wood fibres.

Moose The droppings mostly consist of twigs (red maple is a favourite). In winter, the scat is composed of separate blobs; in summer it looks more like a cow pat.

Red fox The poop contains hair, bones, insects and berry seeds. It's often found on a rock or stump, marking the animal's territory.

Coyote The colour of this scat varies according to the animal's diet, but it usually contains hair, bones and berries.

Black bear The scat contains remnants of animals, nuts, berries, grasses, insects and fish. Bears are omnivorous, and it shows!

African lion Most of what shows in lion scat is fur. This might be from any number of animals, including buffalo, impala, warthogs, wildebeest and zebras.

And what about us humans?
What is the correct outdoor pooping etiquette?
If you are on a camping holiday with friends, **decide on a plan.** There'll be giggles, but you do need some rules.

1 No pooping nearer to camp than 50m (165ft).

2 On a tree branch near the camp, hang a bag containing toilet paper and a small spade. (Then, if the bag is missing, someone is using the woods!)

3 Use the spade to dig a "cat-hole"—just remove about 5cm (2in) of topsoil.

4 When you are done, cover up the poop with a mound of soil, the way a cat does in its litter box. Poop will compost sooner in a shallow trench like this than it will in a deep hole.

5 If you have a strong campfire going, burn your used toilet paper. If not, bury it with the poop. (Maple or other flat leaves are a good substitute loo paper.)

A tall story to tell round the fire
In the Middle Ages, **manure** was a major trading commodity. But it was heavy, due to all the moisture in it, so exporters dried the manure out before loading it onto the wooden ships of the day. In rough seas, water came in through portholes in the cargo holds and this action started the process of **methane production** in the manure. If an unsuspecting seaman went below deck for a quick smoke … **BOOM!!**

So to protect against this, the bales of dried manure were labelled **Store High In Transit** (in other words, on deck in the open air). The stuff still got wet, but the sun dried it off.

Store **H**igh **I**n **T**ransit was soon shortened to its initial letters.

Lost in the desert? Here's what to do

If you are in a car, ask yourself these questions:

Will anyone miss me?
Will they try to come and find me?
Will they notify emergency help or anyone else?

If you said **YES**

1 **Stay where you are,** in the car.

2 **Signal for help.**
The international ground-to-air distress signal is material (anything you can find) arranged in a large V-shape on the ground. At night, if you can, build a number of small fires in this shape.

Another more impressive, but riskier, signal is the tree torch. You must be careful to select a tree that stands alone in an open space.

If you said **NO**

1 **Get moving at night—**
this will help you save energy, and avoid heat and dehydration.

2 **Orient yourself.**
The night sky is your guide.

Note: this will only work for those in the Northern Hemisphere.

3 Now you know which direction is which, **consult your map.**
You do have a map, right?

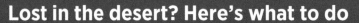

the Big Dipper
(Ursa Major)

An improvised shelter
(This will protect you from sandstorms and the sun.)

Leaves or clothing draped over a twig frame.

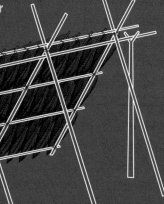

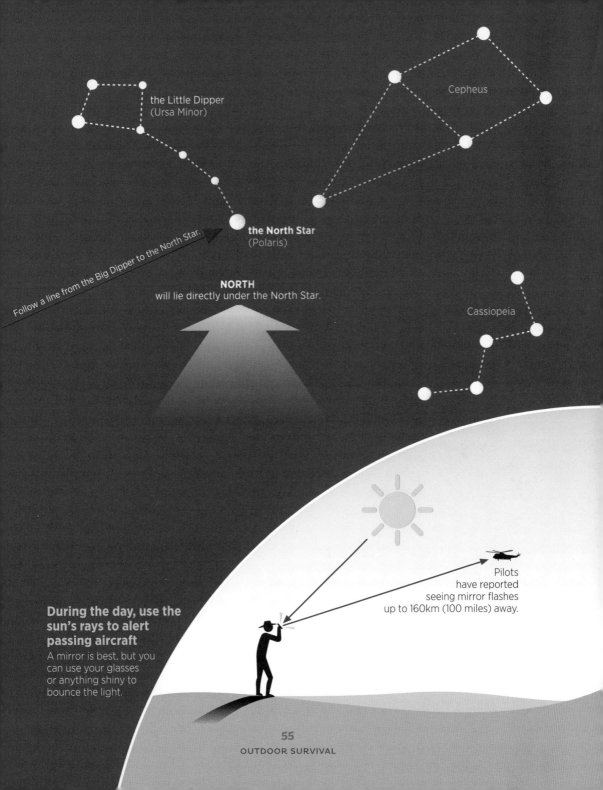

the Little Dipper
(Ursa Minor)

Cepheus

the **North Star**
(Polaris)

Follow a line from the Big Dipper to the North Star.

NORTH
will lie directly under the North Star.

Cassiopeia

During the day, use the sun's rays to alert passing aircraft

A mirror is best, but you can use your glasses or anything shiny to bounce the light.

Pilots have reported seeing mirror flashes up to 160km (100 miles) away.

Lost on a hike: six stages of survival

Psychologists call it "woods shock", and they can predict how you will act when it happens to you. Here are the downs and ups of survival in the wild.

① Disorientation
Which is the right way to go?

Most people keep going forward; few turn round and go back. Returning to the last known place would probably be the best thing for you to do, but at this stage, your denial that anything is really wrong is particularly influential.

② Urgency
The impulse to run

With your surroundings seeming to close in around you, you may try to "break out" from the situation and start running.

③ Panic
Stumbling, and throwing gear away

Thinking that lightening your load will result in extra speed, you'll more than likely discard backpacks, food and other equipment.

If you can find a clear area ...

These are the internationally recognised **ground-to-air signals.** Make them with strips of clothing, foliage—anything you can find that contrasts with the ground. And **make them big** so they can be seen from the air.

1.5m (5ft)

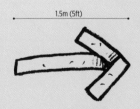

I AM MOVING IN THIS DIRECTION

NEED DOCTOR — SERIOUS INJURY

NEED MEDICAL SUPPLIES

④ Planning
Trying to think of
the way back

Having survived
the initial burst of panic,
some people try to
form a logical plan of
escape. But usually you
are too tired, and by
now are a long way
away from your original
track, so your plans
usually fail.

⑤ Fatigue
Loss of will
to live

The lowest point.
When your plan fails,
you'll be emotionally
and physically drained.
You'll finally admit you
are lost and stop
making any moves to
help yourself, such as
building a shelter
or fire.

⑥ Optimism
Determination and
a sense of humour

The will to live depends
less on equipment (the materials
to make a fire, for instance) than
it does on mental strength.
Thinking about seeing family
and friends again instead of
dwelling on the apparent
hopelessness of the situation
will often pull you through. Try
to keep a sense of humour. Set
small goals; finish them. Build a
shelter. Stay busy. You know
others are looking for you.

NEED FOOD
AND WATER

PROBABLY SAFE
TO LAND HERE

IF IN DOUBT, USE THIS
INTERNATIONAL SYMBOL

Camping tips

Respect for nature and common sense are the hallmarks of good camping. Follow these simple rules for a safer and more enjoyable outdoor trip.

❶ **MOST IMPORTANT:** Select your site **before daylight fades.**

❷ The best protection against lightning is a **stand of medium-sized trees.**

❸ **Set up your kitchen at least 60m (200ft) downwind** from your tent. This will make sure that the remnants of anything edible or fragrant are far away from you at night (bears' supper time).

To prevent pollution, **keep the fire or stove well away from water sources.**

A small stove will do far less harm to the environment than a fire.

❹ Choose a **flat, well-drained site** for the tent. If the soil is compressed or soggy, it will not drain well in case of rain.

Never dig a trench to divert water. If there's a slope to the floor of the tent, make sure you sleep with your head higher than your feet.

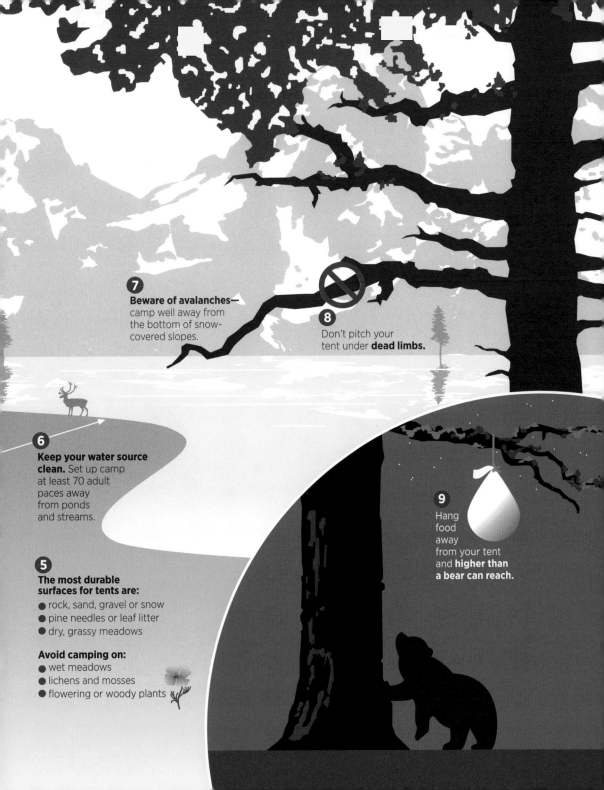

7 **Beware of avalanches—** camp well away from the bottom of snow-covered slopes.

8 Don't pitch your tent under **dead limbs.**

6 **Keep your water source clean.** Set up camp at least 70 adult paces away from ponds and streams.

5 **The most durable surfaces for tents are:**
- rock, sand, gravel or snow
- pine needles or leaf litter
- dry, grassy meadows

Avoid camping on:
- wet meadows
- lichens and mosses
- flowering or woody plants

9 Hang food away from your tent and **higher than a bear can reach.**

The rules of the campfire

Most important: leave the site the way you found it.

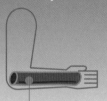

1
Finding fuel
Gather more dry stuff than you think you'll need. You can always put it back where you found it.

The main pieces of wood should be the length of your forearm and about as wide as the diameter of your wrist.

Sticks for **kindling** should be the thickness of a pencil.

Tinder (twigs, dried grass or shredded dry leaves) should be toothpick-sized.

2
Building the fire
Choose a site on exposed bedrock, grass or scattered leaves.

OXYGEN FLOW

Place a **tarp** that's 1m (39in) square at least 3m (10ft) away from dry grass.

Mineral soil 12cm (5in) high, insulates ground and tarp from heat.

Build a **"tepee"** by lodging wood in the mineral soil.

An **opening** allows you to insert tinder and kindling.

3

Lighting the fire
Be prepared. You can never
have enough matches.
(And don't forget to keep them in a
waterproof container.)

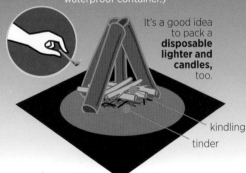

It's a good idea
to pack a
**disposable
lighter and
candles,**
too.

kindling

tinder

**Never light a fire under
an overhanging tree limb;**
the tree could catch fire.

**Or under a rock
overhang;** black smoke will
leave a scar on the rock for years.

4

Clearing up afterwards
The idea is to leave
no trace. Once your fire has
burnt down to ash, clean
up what remains.

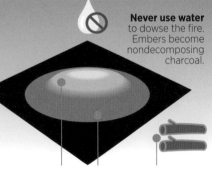

Never use water
to dowse the fire.
Embers become
nondecomposing
charcoal.

**Scatter
the ash.**

**Return
soil**
to its
source.

**Return
leftover
wood** to
the woods,
or take it
with you.

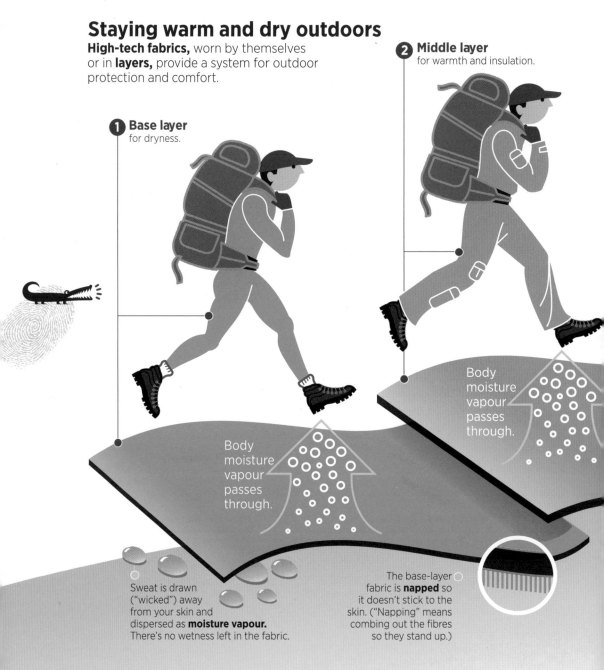

Staying warm and dry outdoors

High-tech fabrics, worn by themselves
or in **layers,** provide a system for outdoor
protection and comfort.

1 Base layer
for dryness.

2 Middle layer
for warmth and insulation.

Body
moisture
vapour
passes
through.

Body
moisture
vapour
passes
through.

Sweat is drawn
("wicked") away
from your skin and
dispersed as **moisture vapour.**
There's no wetness left in the fabric.

The base-layer
fabric is **napped** so
it doesn't stick to the
skin. ("Napping" means
combing out the fibres
so they stand up.)

3 Outer layer for wind- and rain-proofing.

Body moisture vapour passes through.

Insulation is created by tiny gaps ( ) that trap air on both sides of the fabric. Some fleece is made from recycled plastic bottles spun into superthin fibres.

Layers of **bonded microfibres** protect you from the rain and wind: the tight weave of the fabric and a chemical coating produce a water-resistant surface, while the barrier membrane underneath deflects the wind.

How to get out of a sinking car

1

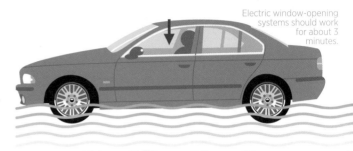

As soon as you realise that you are in water, **open the window.** This will allow water to flow into the car, making the pressure inside the car the same as outside. With equal pressure inside and out, you'll be able to open the door. Your car might float for a short time, but don't count on it.

Electric window-opening systems should work for about 3 minutes.

2

If the most of the door is above the water level, you might be able to open it, but if not, **leave the door alone.** (You'll only have seconds before outside water pressure means that you can't open it anyway.) Don't try to to use your mobile phone. You do not have time.

3

Unbuckle your seat belt. Leaving a seat belt on might give you leverage when it's time to open the door (see **6**), but experts seem to agree that it is more important to be able to move around without your seat belt restraining you.

4

If the car has a front-mounted engine, it will go down at a steep angle. If you cannot open the window, try to **break the glass with a heavy object.** If you have a hammer, a laptop, steering-wheel lock or even an umbrella, aim it at the centre of the glass. You could also try **kicking the window out,** by aiming your heel at the front of it. Don't bother trying to break the windshield: it's made of unbreakable glass.

Take a deep breath and swim out through the broken window. It will be a struggle because you are swimming against a strong inflow of water.

If you have still failed to open the window, wait until the car has almost filled with water. As it rises up to your nose, **take a deep breath and hold your nose.** When the car is full, (total time will be 1–2 minutes), the water will be over your head, the pressure of water will be the same on the inside of the car as the outside, and you will be able to open the door.

If the water is more than about 4.5m (15ft) deep, your car might flip over. Of course, that will make it much harder to get out, and that's why **you must act quickly.**

ETIQUETTE

How to kiss!

It differs from country to country,
so make sure you know where you are.

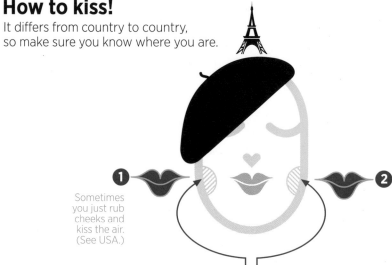

Sometimes
you just rub
cheeks and
kiss the air.
(See USA.)

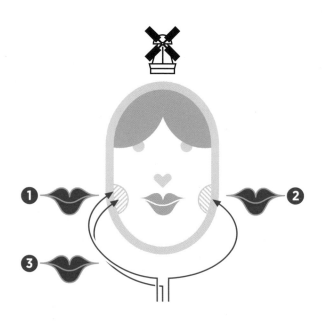

Other worldly ways to say hello

Basic rule: **check with the locals** about what's done (and not done).

Here are a few pointers:

In the **United Arab Emirates,** men kiss other men three to four times on the cheeks.

In **Saudi Arabia,** men kiss on both cheeks after shaking hands.

In **Spain,** it's the same as in France, but you go to the right side first.

In **Africa,** some people kiss the ground when tribal leaders have just passed by.

Not much kissing in the **U.K.** Just shake hands there.

Same thing in **Germany.**

Here you really kiss the air.

Oh behave! (in England)

During your trip to London, you might get invited to Buckingham Palace. (OK, let's *pretend* you might get invited to Buckingham Palace.)

This is how to
curtsey to the Queen
when you meet her.
Please practise, because she does expect it.

The Queen doesn't actually wear a crown all the time, but lots of people would like it if she did.

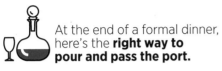

At the end of a formal dinner, here's the **right way to pour and pass the port.**

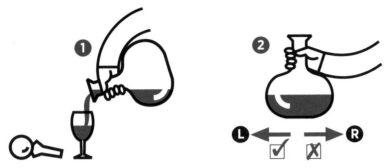

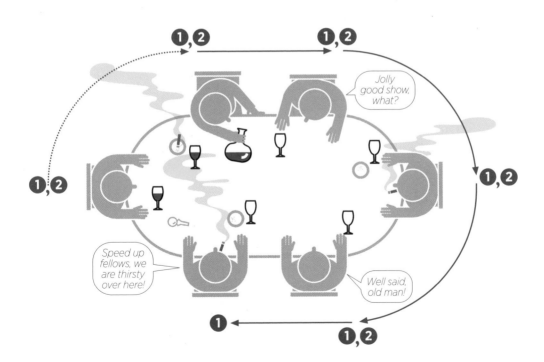

How to use chopsticks

Chopsticks originated in China in the Shang Dynasty (1600–1046 BC) and were first used for cooking—the earliest ones found were bronze—not as eating utensils. In China, Taiwan, Japan, Korea and Vietnam there are variations in styles, materials and etiquette, but here's a basic guide to holding them, with some facts about history and manners.

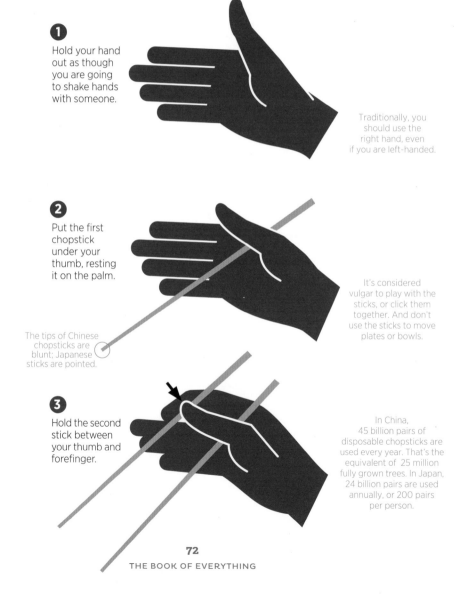

1 Hold your hand out as though you are going to shake hands with someone.

Traditionally, you should use the right hand, even if you are left-handed.

2 Put the first chopstick under your thumb, resting it on the palm.

It's considered vulgar to play with the sticks, or click them together. And don't use the sticks to move plates or bowls.

The tips of Chinese chopsticks are blunt; Japanese sticks are pointed.

3 Hold the second stick between your thumb and forefinger.

In China, 45 billion pairs of disposable chopsticks are used every year. That's the equivalent of 25 million fully grown trees. In Japan, 24 billion pairs are used annually, or 200 pairs per person.

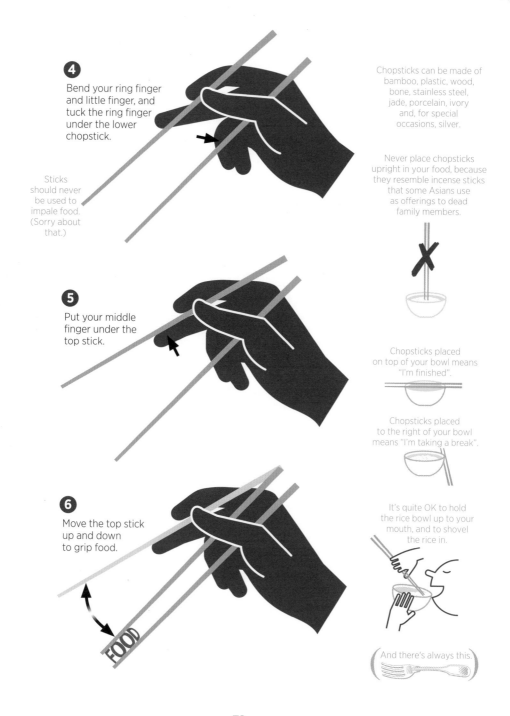

4

Bend your ring finger and little finger, and tuck the ring finger under the lower chopstick.

Sticks should never be used to impale food. (Sorry about that.)

Chopsticks can be made of bamboo, plastic, wood, bone, stainless steel, jade, porcelain, ivory and, for special occasions, silver.

Never place chopsticks upright in your food, because they resemble incense sticks that some Asians use as offerings to dead family members.

5

Put your middle finger under the top stick.

Chopsticks placed on top of your bowl means "I'm finished".

Chopsticks placed to the right of your bowl means "I'm taking a break".

6

Move the top stick up and down to grip food.

FOOD

It's quite OK to hold the rice bowl up to your mouth, and to shovel the rice in.

And there's always this.

How to wear a kilt

Everyone wants to know: **underpants or no underpants?** Sorry to squish a lovely story, but it's a myth that kilt wearers go without underneath. And since the formal kilt (the outfit shown here) is often worn where wild and informal dancing is likely to break out, wearing them is a good way to avoid embarrassment.

A white wing-collar **shirt** and black **bow tie** are worn on formal occasions.

Traditional, formal **Prince Charlie jacket** and **waistcoat**.

The **belt** goes through kilt loops at the back.

The chain securing the **sporran** also goes through the kilt loops.

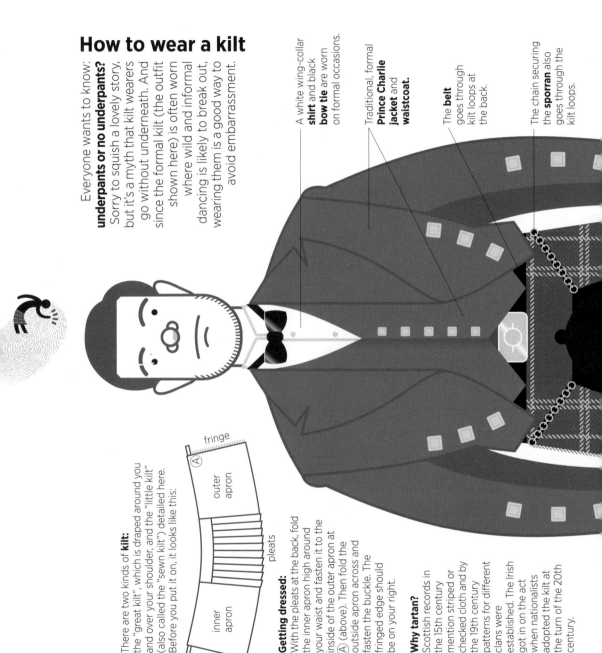

There are two kinds of **kilt:** the "great kilt", which is draped around you and over your shoulder, and the "little kilt" (also called the "sewn kilt") detailed here. Before you put it on, it looks like this:

fringe

Ⓐ

outer apron

inner apron

pleats

Getting dressed:
With the pleats at the back, fold the inner apron high around your waist and fasten it to the inside of the outer apron at Ⓐ (above). Then fold the outside apron across and fasten the buckle. The fringed edge should be on your right.

Why tartan?
Scottish records in the 15th century mention striped or checked cloth and by the 19th century patterns for different clans were established. The Irish got in on the act when nationalists adopted the kilt at the turn of the 20th century.

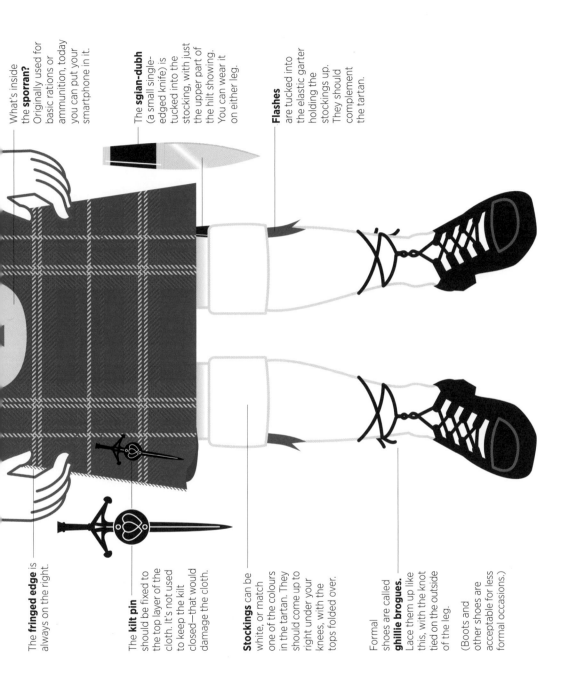

What's inside the **sporran?** Originally used for basic rations or ammunition, today you can put your smartphone in it.

The **sgian-dubh** (a small single-edged knife) is tucked into the stocking, with just the upper part of the hilt showing. You can wear it on either leg.

Flashes are tucked into the elastic garter holding the stockings up. They should complement the tartan.

The **fringed edge** is always on the right.

The **kilt pin** should be fixed to the top layer of the cloth. It's not used to keep the kilt closed—that would damage the cloth.

Stockings can be white, or match one of the colours in the tartan. They should come up to right under your knees, with the tops folded over.

Formal shoes are called **ghillie brogues.** Lace them up like this, with the knot tied on the outside of the leg.

(Boots and other shoes are acceptable for less formal occasions.)

Cultural no-nos

Other people's social customs can be very different from yours. Here are some pitfalls to watch out for.

OOPS!

Your job?

It's rude to ask people in **Argentina** what they do for a living. Wait until they want to bring it up in conversation.

Aaaatchoo!

In **Japan,** never blow your nose into a handkerchief. The Japanese word for snot is *hanakuso*, which translates to "nose shit", so they don't like the idea of anyone carrying it around with them.

Giving flowers? Watch out!

Carnations are used at funerals in **Germany, Poland** and **Sweden.** Chrysanthemums are used at funerals in **Belgium, Italy, France, Spain** and **Turkey.**

Giving flowers? Part two

It's unlucky to give odd numbers of flowers in **China** and **Indonesia,** but odd numbers of flowers are lucky in **Germany, India, Russia** and **Turkey.**

Gloves off

In **Europe,** you'll be considered rude if you don't take your gloves off before shaking hands. (Even if it's freezing outside!)

The bill

In restaurants in **Spain,** always request the bill at the end of a meal. Waiters think it's rude to bring it to you before you have asked for it.

Eye level

In **Scandinavia** and **Germany** you should look your fellow travellers in the eye when you are toasting. In **Russia,** drink the vodka in one gulp.

Head matters

At holy places in **Thailand** and other Buddhist countries, never pat anyone on the head. The head is sacred.

Thumbing

The thumbs up sign is a rude gesture in **Egypt** and **Iran.**

 No thanks

As much as you might have enjoyed a meal in **India,** don't thank the host because saying "thank you" is seen as a form of payment, and may be taken as an insult.

 Foot blunder

In most of **Asia,** feet are thought of as being dirty, so it's disrespectful to point your feet or show the bottom of your shoes to anyone. Don't do it!

 Right is right

The left hand is considered the dirty hand in **Africa** and **India,** so use only your right hand when you eat.

 Palming

When getting a taxi in **Greece,** don't raise your hand as you would to signal *stop.* Greeks consider the forward-facing palm to be offensive, so turn your hand so that the palm is towards you (and keep the fingers together).

 Never leather

In **India,** don't give anyone a present made of leather, because cows are sacred. Also many people in India are vegetarian and may be offended by your gift.

 I didn't mean that!

In the **Philippines,** never refer to someone who has invited you to an event as your "hostess": it means "prostitute".

 Reading the cards

If you are on business in **Japan,** the business card exchange is a ritual you need to know about. Receive the card with both hands and a slight bow, then read it carefully. Never put it into your pocket or write on it.

 Wink, wink

Never wink at anyone in **India,** unless you know that it has sexual connotations!

How to visit a mosque

There are just a few rules, but it's very important that you respect them.

 Check ahead if non-Muslims may enter; some mosques may not always be open to non-Muslims. Friday is the day when it's most likely that you will not be allowed to visit. In certain cases, non-Muslims may have restricted access, or may not be allowed to enter at all.

(If you can't enter, you might be able to get a view of the mosque from elsewhere.)

Avoid entering during the calls to prayer (five times daily) unless you are a Muslim.

 Dress modestly—no shorts are allowed, and both men and women should cover their arms and backs.

Men should wear trousers, **not jeans.** Women must **cover their hair** with a headscarf, and wear a long skirt. Some mosques ask women to put on a cloak. (Headscarves and cloaks, if required, are usually provided.)

 Remove your shoes. Check at which point you should do this; as a general rule that will be when entering carpeted areas or the prayer hall.

 If you sit on the carpet, **make sure your feet are tucked behind you**—it is offensive to Muslims to have the soles of your feet pointed at them.

 Photos: check if you are allowed to use your camera and if you can, be discreet.

 Don't smoke.

 Take care not to touch the Quran.

What is the "muezzin's call"?

- The muezzin is the chosen person at the mosque to summon Muslims to prayer at Friday services and the five daily times for prayer—at dawn, noon, midafternoon, sunset and nightfall (about two hours after sunset).

- The muezzin faces the direction of Mecca as he delivers the call from the minaret.

- The office of muezzin in cities is sometimes given to a blind man who cannot see down into the inner courtyards of citizens' houses, thus avoiding any possibility of intrusion into people's privacy.

- In most modern mosques the call (*adhan*) is electronically amplified.

- Egypt has introduced a controversial centralised muezzin: a single voice is broadcast live to the 4,500 mosques in Cairo.

The call

" *Allah is most great. I testify that there is no God but Allah. I testify that Muhammad is the prophet of Allah. Come to prayer. Come to salvation. Allah is most great. There is no God but Allah.* **"**

The melodious chanting of the *adhan* is considered an art form.

Want some fun?

When it comes to a holiday romance, you'll do a lot better if you ask nicely and in the right language. Here's **how to chat people up (and turn them down)!**

 In French:

Do you want to go out with me?
Veux-tu sortir avec moi?
ver•tew sor•teer a•vek mwa

I love you.
Je t'aime.
zher•tem

Would you like to do something?
Est-ce que tu aimerais faire quelque chose?
es•ker tew em•ray fair kel•ker shoz

Yes, I'd love to.
Oui, j'aimerais bien.
wee zhem•ray byun

Would you like a drink?
Si on buvait quelque chose?
see on bew•vay kel•ker shoz

Shall we get some fresh air?
Nous allons prendre l'air?
noo za•lon pron•drer lair

Leave me alone, please.
Laissez-moi tranquille, s'il vous plaît.
lay•say•mwa trong•keel seel voo play

I'm sorry, I can't.
Non, je suis désolé(e), je ne peux pas.
non zher swee day•zo•lay zher ner per pa

Not if you were the last person on earth!
Jamais de la vie!
zha•may der la vee

I like you very much.
Je t'aime beaucoup.
zher tem bo•koo

You're very attractive.
Tu es trés beau/belle.
tew ay tray bo/bel

I'm interested in you.
Je m'intéresse vraiment á toi.
zher mun•tay•res vray•mon a twa

You're great.
Tu es formidable.
tew ay for•mee•da•bler

Let's go to bed!
On va se coucher!
on va ser koo•shay

Kiss me.
Embrasse-moi.
om•bras•mwa

Excuse me, I have to go now.
Excusez-moi, je dois partir maintenant.
ek•skyew•zay•mwa zher dwa par•teer mun•ter•non

No, thank you.
Non, merci.
non mair•see

I'd rather not.
Je n'ai pas trés envie.
zher nay pa tray zon•vee

 In Russian:

Would you like to do something?
kha•tit•ye peyd•yom ku•da•ni•butí

I love you.
ya lyub•lyu tib•ya

Would you like a drink?
kha•tit•ye vih•pití sa mnoy

What are you having?
shto vih kha•tit•ye pití

You look great!
vih klas•na vih•gli•dit•ye

I want to get to know you better.
mnye bih khat•ye•lasí uz•natí a tib•ye pa•bolí•she

Can I kiss you?
mozh•na tib•ya pat•se•la•vatí

Do you want to come inside for a while?
kho•chishí zey•ti na vryem•ya

Can I stay over?
mozh•na mnye a•statí•sa

Kiss me.
pat•se•luy min•ya

Let's go to bed.
da•vey f past•yelí

Excuse me, I have to go now.
iz•vi•nit•ye mnye pa•ra i•ti

Leave me alone!
pri•va•li•vey

Sorry, I can't.
sa•zhal•ye•ni•yu ya nye ma•gu

Piss off!
at•ye•bisí

In Italian:

I love you.
Ti amo.
tee a•mo

Would you like a drink?
Prendi qualcosa da bere?
pren•dee kwal•ko•za da be•re

Can I dance with you?
Posso ballare con te?
po•so ba•la•re kon te

Shall we get some fresh air?
Andiamo a prendere
un po'd'aria fresca?
an•dya•mo a pren•de•re
oon po da•rya fres•ka

Can I sit here?
Posso sedermi qui?
po•so se•der•mee kwee

Can I kiss you?
Ti posso baciare?
tee po•so ba•cha•re

Will you take me home?
Mi porti a casa?
mee por•tee a ka•za

Let's go to bed!
Andiamo a letto!
an•dya•mo a le•to

**I'm sorry, but I
don't feel like it.**
Mi dispiace ma
non ne ho voglia.
mee dees•pya•che ma
non ne o vo•lya

I'm not interested.
Non mi interessa.
non mee een•te•re•sa

Leave me alone!
Lasciami in pace!
la•sha• mee een pa•che

In German:

Haven't we met before?
Kennen wir uns nicht von
irgendwoher?
ke•nen veer uns nikht fon
ir•gent•vo•hair

Would you like a drink?
Möchtest du etwas trinken?
merkh•test doo et•vas
tring•ken

**You have a beautiful
personality.**
Du hast eine wundervolle
Persönlichkeit.
doo hast ai•ne vun•der•
vo•ler per•zern•likh•kait

Kiss me.
Küss mich.
kus mikh

Let's go to bed!
Gehen wir ins Bett!
gay•en veer ins bet

**Excuse me, I have
to go now.**
Tut mir Leid, ich muss
jetzt gehen.
toot meer lait ikh mus
yetst gay•en

No, thank you.
Nein, danke.
nain dang•ke

I'd rather not.
Lieber nicht.
lee•ber nikht

Perhaps some other time.
Vielleicht ein andermal.
fi•laikht ain an•der•mahl

Leave me alone!
Lass mich zufrieden!
las mikh tsu•free•den

In Spanish:

Would you like to do something?
¿Quieres hacer algo?
kye•res a•ther al•go

I love you.
Te quiero.
te kye•ro

Would you like a drink?
¿Te apetece una copa?
te a•pe•te•the oo•na ko•pa

You're great.
Eres estupendo/a.
e•res es•too•pen•do/a

Can I kiss you?
¿Te puedo besar?
te pwe•do b••sar

**Do you want to come
inside for a drink?**
¿Quieres entrar a tomar algo?
kye•res en•trar a to•mar al•go

Let's go to bed!
¡V·monos a la cama!
va•mo•nos a la ka•ma

Excuse me, I have to go now.
Lo siento, pero me tengo que ir.
lo syen•to pe•ro me ten•go
ke eer

Leave me alone, please.
Déjame en paz, por favor.
de•kha•me en path por fa•vor

Go away!
¡Vete!
ve•te

**Hey, I'm not interested in
talking to you.**
Mira tĺo/a, es que no me
interesa hablar contigo.
mee•ra tee•o/a es ke no me
een•te•re•sa ab•lar kon•tee•go

Tipping tips

These are just guidelines, because tipping experts have differing opinions about some of the details. **Best advice: ask a local.** Unless you are on a really tight budget, why not give the waiter something when he or she is nice to you, even if this list suggests you don't have to. It's friendly to say thank you.

Restaurants Taxis Typically not required Typically included Loose change Highest Lowest

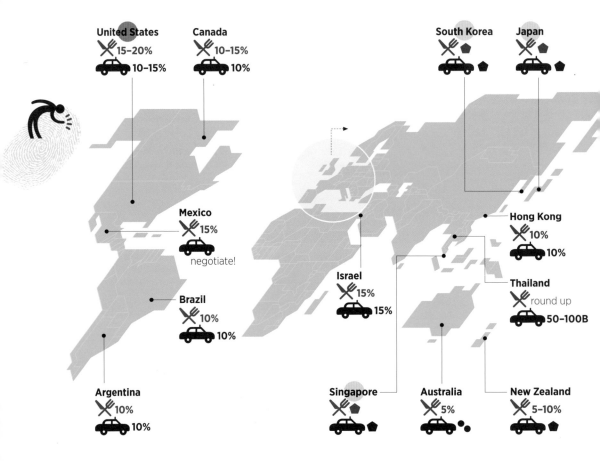

United States
15–20%
10–15%

Canada
10–15%
10%

South Korea

Japan

Mexico
15%
negotiate!

Hong Kong
10%
10%

Israel
15%
15%

Thailand
round up
50–100B

Brazil
10%
10%

Argentina
10%
10%

Singapore

Australia
5%

New Zealand
5–10%

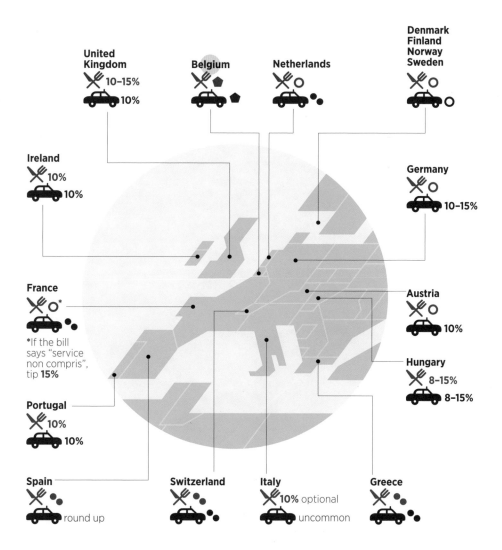

United Kingdom
10–15%
10%

Belgium

Netherlands

**Denmark
Finland
Norway
Sweden**

Ireland
10%
10%

Germany
10–15%

France
o*

*If the bill
says "service
non compris",
tip **15%**

Austria
10%

Hungary
8–15%
8–15%

Portugal
10%
10%

Spain
round up

Switzerland

Italy
10% optional
uncommon

Greece

MEDICAL

AARRGHH! My back's killing me!

You do know that travelling can be exhausting, don't you? Even so, sooner or later you'll overdo it, and often the first thing to give you trouble is your back. No gym or fitness centre is needed for these simple exercises.

Do them gently at first. If you continue with them regularly (even when there's no pain) you'll strengthen the muscles in your back, and there'll be less chance you'll have back problems on future trips.

1 Stand against a wall with your feet slightly forward.

2 Slide down (and back up) slowly.

Repeat a few times.

1 Sit up straight.

2 Reach as far as you can.

1 Kneel on floor.

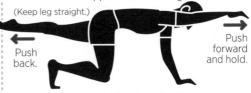

2 Stretch forward and back with opposite arm and leg.

(Keep leg straight.)

Push back.

Push forward and hold.

Repeat on both sides a few times.

1 Lie on your back with knees bent; raise torso.

2 Bring knee to opposite elbow.

Repeat on both sides, in a continuous back-and-forth flow.

(Pointed toes do not touch floor.)

1 Lie flat on tummy and raise torso.

2 Raise whole body to "plank" position off the floor. Hold for a few seconds and repeat.

(Keep legs straight.)

How to carry an injured friend from a remote location

Accidents will happen. Here are five ways to transport the patient safely.

But if the injury has knocked the person out so they cannot be carried by one of these methods, you can make a pretty good stretcher out of blankets and strong sticks.

1
Grab your partner's arms to make a secure seat **like this.**

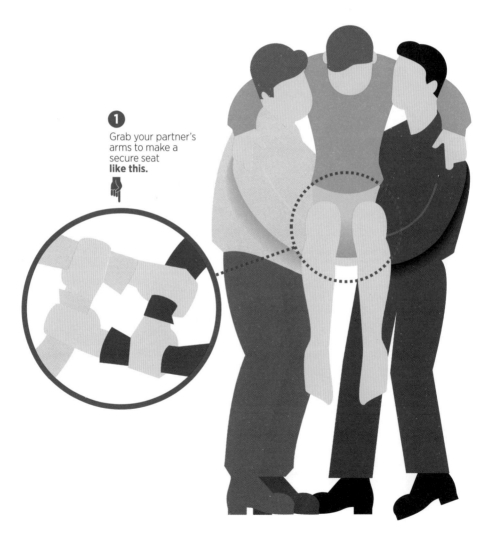

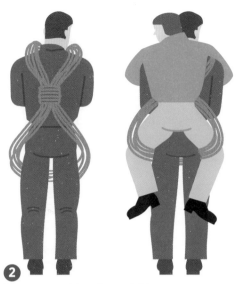

2 Tie your ropes into a figure eight.

3 If it's a long walk back to base, cut the bottom out of your backpack. It makes a workable adult version of a baby sling.

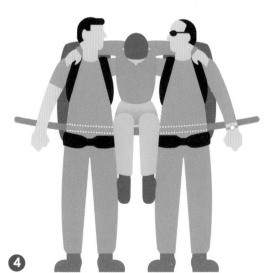

4 Slot a strong walking stick or thin branch through your backpack straps to make a seat.

5 Try the classic fireman's lift.

Vitaminology *(if that's a word)*

You should be getting all the vitamins your body needs by eating a balanced diet. But when you are travelling that can be difficult. Check out what you might be missing.

year discovered **1913**

generic name (letter) **A**

chemical name **retinol**

lack can lead to night blindness, eye disorders

good sources orange and yellow fruits, leafy vegetables, carrots, pumpkin, squash, spinach, liver, cod liver oil

1931 B5

pantothenic acid

paresthesia (skin numbness)

meat, broccoli, avocados, whole grains

1934 B6

pyridoxine

anaemia (blood disorders, fatigue)

meat, vegetables, tree nuts, bananas, dairy products

1931 B7

biotin

dermatitis (eczema)

raw egg yolk, peanuts, liver

1920 D

calciferol (D$_2$); cholecalciferol (D$_3$)

rickets (softening of bones)

fish, eggs, mushrooms, milk, liver, cod liver oil, sunshine

1922 E

deficiency very rare

tocopherol

poor blood cell and tissue heath

unrefined vegetable oils, wheat germ oil

1929 K

phylloquinone (K$_1$); menaquinone (K$_2$)

bleeding diathesis (susceptibility to bleeding)

leafy green vegetables, egg yolks, liver

1910

B₁

thiamine

beriberi (fatigue)

pork, oatmeal, brown rice, bran, vegetables, liver, eggs

1920

B₂

riboflavin

ariboflavinosis (sore throat, mouth swelling, cracked lips)

dairy products, bananas, popcorn, green beans, asparagus

1936

B₃

niacin

pellagra (sensitivity to sun, dermatitis, dementia, skin lesions)

meat, fish, eggs, mushrooms, tree nuts

1941

B₉

folic acid

megaloblast (birth defects during pregnancy)

leafy vegetables, pasta, bread, cereal, liver

1926

B₁₂

cobalamin

megaloblastic anaemia (blood disorders)

meat, eggs

1920

C

ascorbic acid

scurvy (lethargy, bone pain, easy bruising)

citrus and other fruit, vegetables, liver

Since **liver** seems to be the winning vitaminizer *(another new word?),* it seems right to give you a recipe for it:

● Calf's liver is best. Peel off the membrane, and cut into quarter-inch slices.

● Season with salt and pepper; coat with flour.

● Heat 2 tablespoons of vegetable oil or butter in a skillet over medium-high heat.

 medium-high

● Brown the liver quickly on both sides (only about 1–2 minutes; overcooking will turn it to leather!).

 1–2 minutes

Liver is good with onions. Slice them thinly; cook over low heat until soft (20+ minutes).

CPR: **we should all know how to do this**

Cardio-
Pulmonary
Resuscitation
= reviving
the heart
and lungs

1 **Call emergency services.**

2 If the victim is not
breathing normally,
nor coughing
or moving,
**start chest
pumping.**

Push down,
in the centre
of the chest
**5cm (2in),
30 times.**

Keep going **hard and fast.**
You should be pumping at least
100 times a minute, faster
than once a second.

(Continue until there are
signs of movement, or until
emergency medical personnel
take over.)

This might seem
like a lot. You
may actually break
ribs doing this. But
remember, you are
saving a life here;
ribs can be mended,
death cannot.

5cm (2in)

Continuous, hard
chest pumping
is considered
to be the most
important part
of CPR.

Recently, health experts found that many people were not engaging in **mouth-to-mouth resuscitation** for fear of disease, or just because they were squeamish about doing it. Unfortunately, they also found that most people doing CPR were not pumping the chest hard or long enough. Therefore, CPR guidelines now place less emphasis on mouth-to-mouth, and more on pumping.

In fact, it is highly unlikely that you will get a disease from performing mouth-to-mouth, and filling the lungs up with air is important. So here's what you do:

③ **Tilt the victim's head back** and listen for possible sounds of coughing or vomiting. (One result of pumping the chest is that the victim vomits. Turn the head to the side, and try to wipe the liquid out of the way.)

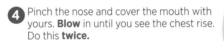

④ Pinch the nose and cover the mouth with yours. **Blow** in until you see the chest rise. Do this **twice.**

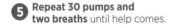

⑤ **Repeat 30 pumps and two breaths** until help comes.

⑥ Two people giving CPR is good: one pumping, one blowing air in. (Take turns, do not do both at once.)

Beating jetlag

The tiredness you feel is your body's reaction to crossing time zones.
(A contributing factor is the stress of travelling in general.)
What you need to do is **reset your internal clock.**

BEFORE YOU GO

1 Try to **shift your sleep pattern.** Go to bed one hour earlier or later depending on which direction you are flying—but no more than 1 hour per night—for as many time zones as you are going to cross (or as many as you can manage).

2 If you are going on a really long flight (for instance, from Europe to Australia) take **melatonin** for 2–3 days before the trip.
For shorter trips, don't take it before you go. See "When you arrive" for when to use it.

Melatonin is a sleep-inducing hormone that occurs naturally in your brain and it controls the body's daily rhythm. You can buy it without a prescription. It is available up to 3mg, but a lower dose (0.5mg) has been found to have the same effect. So less is better.

3 **Ginger tea** is thought to be a good way to counteract jetlag.
Here's a quick recipe:
- Boil water.
- Grate 2 teaspoons of fresh ginger (*much* better than powdered ginger) into a cup.
- Add boiling water.
- Allow to steep for 5 minutes.

Ideally you should drink it at the start of your trip, an hour before you take off, but often that's not possible. Instead, you might take a small piece of fresh ginger to **chew** on the plane—but beware, it's hot and spicy!

Jetlag is less pronounced when you travel **west,** and gain hours.

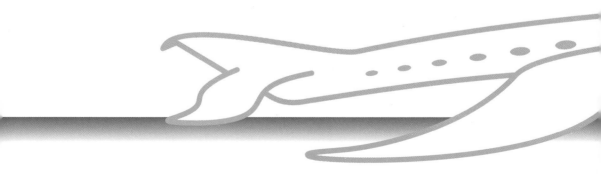

ON THE PLANE

1 **Go to sleep** as soon as possible. Wear loose clothing, a mask and earplugs.

2 **Don't take sleeping pills.** They will interfere with your sleep pattern when you arrive at your destination.

3 **Don't drink alcohol or coffee.** They dehydrate you and that emphasises the effects of jetlag, because your body is stressed by being dried out. Just drink water.

Jetlag is worse when you travel **east,** and lose hours.

WHEN YOU ARRIVE

1 Flying east or west, **stay up until it's bedtime** wherever you are.

2 **Walk around** in the sun. Here's hoping you are not in England in the winter or Seattle, USA, at any time. (Just kidding, Seattle.) If you must nap, make it for no more than an hour.

3 If you flew eastward, take a low dose of **melatonin** for 3 nights before bed.

If you flew westward, and find yourself waking up early the first morning there, take a low dose of melatonin.

In general, the time it takes for your body to adjust is **1 day for every time zone** you've crossed. You may not have time for that!

Travelling exercises

How to keep in shape while you're waiting for a plane, and when you're on board (or in a car, or a train).

BACK EXTENSIONS WHILE STANDING ...

Place both hands on your back at waist level. With your chin tucked in, slowly arch your upper body backwards and hold the position. Slowly straighten ypur back into an upright position. Relax and repeat.

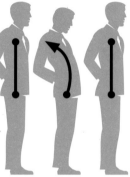

AND SEATED

Position your hands on your back at the waist. Arch your upper body backward while tucking in your chin. Hold and repeat.

LEG STRETCHES

While sitting, interlock the fingers of both hands and grasp your shin just below the knee. Then slowly pull the leg toward your chest. Hold. Repeat with your other leg.

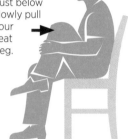

MORE LEG STRETCHES

Place one foot in front of the other and bend the forward knee while keeping the other leg straight. Lean forward and hold. Repeat with your other leg.

HEEL LIFT

Lift one heel as high as possible, but keep toes on the floor. Repeat with other foot.

FOOT FLEX

Lift toes up as far as you can, but keep heels on the floor. Relax and repeat.

SHOULDER ROLLS

Holding your arms at your side, slowly roll your shoulders both forward and backwards in wide circular motions. Repeat.

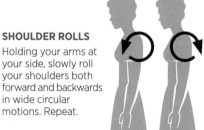

EYE ROTATIONS

Move your eyes slowly in all directions: clockwise, anticlockwise, side to side and up and down.

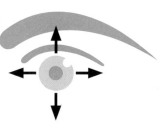

SHOULDER STRETCHES

Place right hand on your left shoulder. Then, using your left hand, push up on right elbow and hold. Do the same with the left hand placed on the right shoulder. Repeat twice with each arm.

HAND, FINGER AND WRIST STRETCHES

First make a fist with both hands; then spread all fingers outward. Relax and repeat.

Especially important for computer and smartphone users!

DEEP BREATHING

Slowly inhale through your nose. Hold the breath for two seconds, then exhale through your mouth. Repeat.

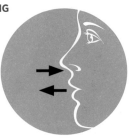

NECK TURNS

Holding your head upright, slowly turn it to one side and hold. Then slowly turn your head to the other side and hold. Next, slowly tip your head forward and hold.

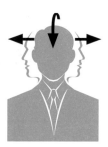

Exercises without equipment

When travelling, you need to keep fit and flexible so you can enjoy the sights (and the food). Try these simple moves in your hotel room or on the beach.

① **Child's pose** Kneel and rest your hips on your heels. Touch head to floor and hold for up to 5 minutes.

② **Shoulder stretch** Lie on belly, and stretch arms out to side. Raise them just off the ground. Hold, then lower.

③ **Cat stretch** Inhale and raise chin and tailbone, so the spine curves downwards. Then exhale and arch the spine upwards. Repeat 10 times.

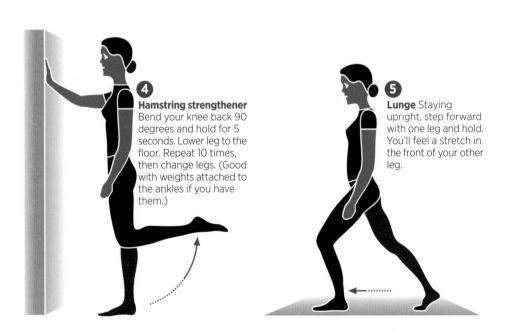

④ **Hamstring strengthener** Bend your knee back 90 degrees and hold for 5 seconds. Lower leg to the floor. Repeat 10 times, then change legs. (Good with weights attached to the ankles if you have them.)

⑤ **Lunge** Staying upright, step forward with one leg and hold. You'll feel a stretch in the front of your other leg.

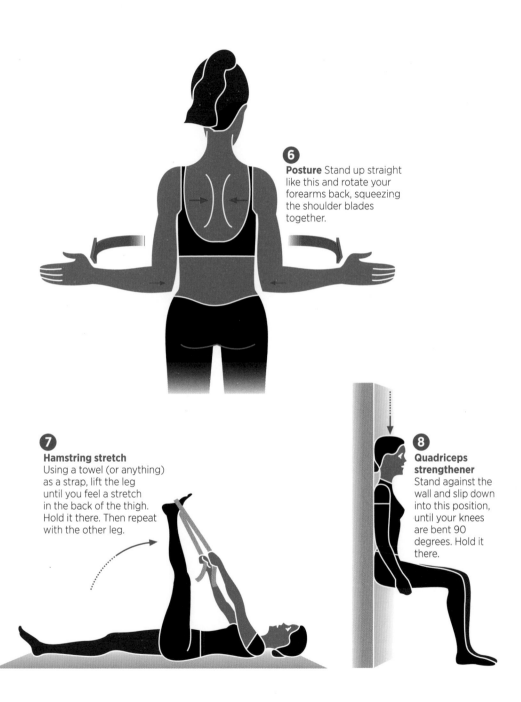

6 **Posture** Stand up straight like this and rotate your forearms back, squeezing the shoulder blades together.

7 **Hamstring stretch** Using a towel (or anything) as a strap, lift the leg until you feel a stretch in the back of the thigh. Hold it there. Then repeat with the other leg.

8 **Quadriceps strengthener** Stand against the wall and slip down into this position, until your knees are bent 90 degrees. Hold it there.

More moves without (real) exercise equipment

For instance, this could be a beach bucket with some sand in it, or a heavy book.

1

Lunging with some resistance

A
Step forward with one leg. (Both knees should be bent.)

B
After swinging the bucket across your body, return it to the original position as you step forward with your other leg. Continue moving forward like this.

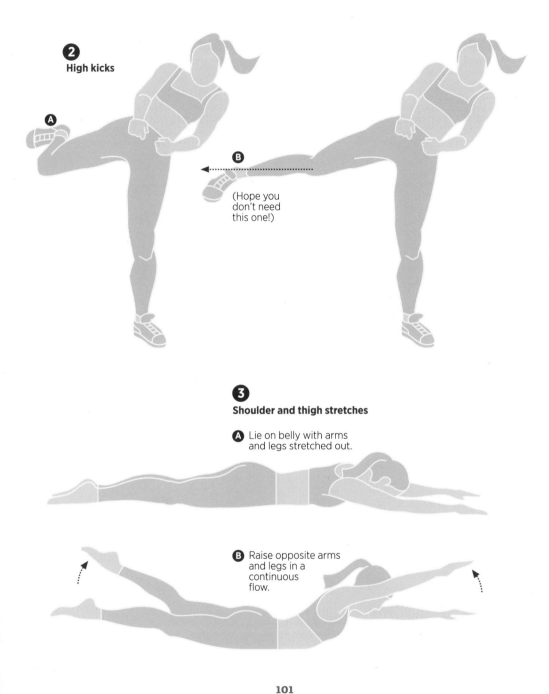

2
High kicks

Ⓐ

Ⓑ

(Hope you
don't need
this one!)

3
Shoulder and thigh stretches

Ⓐ Lie on belly with arms
and legs stretched out.

Ⓑ Raise opposite arms
and legs in a
continuous
flow.

Sun safety

Be a wise traveller; use these protective measures.

Hat
Wear a light-coloured one—
floppy or straw.

Wide all-around brim
Shading cheeks, ears and neck.

When you are driving
UV rays shine right through glass.
Apply an extra dollop of "drive-side"
protection to your arm, and the
side of your face closest to the
window, as well as both
hands on the driving wheel.

Sunglasses and eyes
Must have 100% UV protection.
Don't forget your eyelids. Find a
sunscreen that's opthalmologist
tested and fragrance free.

Lips
Since they have no melanin,
lips need special care. Buy a
waterproof sunscreen just for
them, clear enough to wear up
and over the lip line.

Perfume
It can cause a photo-
chemical reaction on skin.
Attracts bees, too.

Clothes
Protective covering *should*
include long-sleeved, tightly
woven, pale-coloured cover-ups,
that are loose fitting for comfort.

So walk around like this —
at your own risk. It does
look good, though!

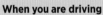

Medicine
Some prescriptions (topical
and nontopical) can cause
photosensitivity. Play safe.
Check with your pharmacist.

Exposure time  = 1 hour

Sun exposure is cumulative. The rays you soak up, add up. Here are some typical exposure times for different activities. Make sure you have enough sunscreen, and that you use it liberally and often!

Watching a football game

Playing nine holes of golf

Window shopping

A day working in an office by the window

Eating lunch outdoors

Gardening

Jogging at noon

Skiing all day

Pushing a baby carriage, or a swing

Waterskiing

Walking the dog

Sun stuff

From SPF to UVA and UVB, what's an acronym-challenged traveller to do?

1 **What's in the sun's rays?**

The parts of a sunbeam that most affect your skin are the **ultraviolet rays A and B,** and **infrared** rays.

These are the rays that can cause skin cancer.

These are the burning rays that turn your skin red, and may also affect its DNA.

These penetrate deep into the skin and damage its support structure. They inhibit the repair of UVB injury, cause changes in blood vessels and are responsible for premature skin ageing.

UVA
UVB
INFRARED

2 **The sun's bounce-back effect**

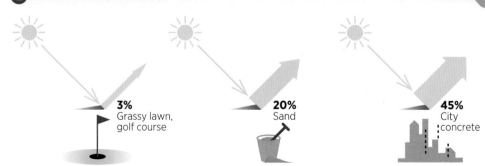

3%
Grassy lawn, golf course

20%
Sand

45%
City concrete

❸ What exactly is "SPF"?

It stands for Sun Protection Factor. The **number** (that follows "SPF") is a multiple of the amount of sun time it would normally take your skin to start to burn **without protection.**

So, if you start to redden within **10 minutes** ...

you should apply a **SPF 15** sunscreen ...

and you'll be protected for **2.5 hours.**

10 minutes x 15 minutes = 150 minutes (2.5 hours)

Remember: **the higher the SPF, the greater the protection.**
SPF 15 is the lowest number recommended by most dermatologists.
SPF 30 is generally agreed to be the maximum required if you have a fair complexion, red hair or lots of freckles. (If you have all three, go up to SPF 50.)
Note: many sunscreens do not block UVA radiation. Use a broad-spectrum (UVA/UVB) sunscreen to address this.

❹ Be careful in the sun

Try to avoid the sun completely during these hours:

10am–2pm

take a siesta instead!

(During daylight saving time, that's 11am–3pm.)

During these hours, avoid the sun if you are ...

10am–3pm

in higher altitudes ...

or near the equator.

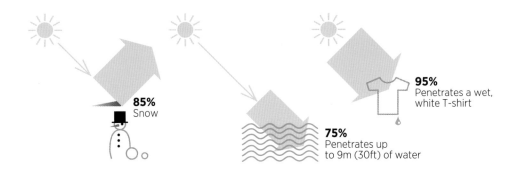

85%
Snow

75%
Penetrates up to 9m (30ft) of water

95%
Penetrates a wet, white T-shirt

Dealing with snakebites

Most snakes kill their prey with constriction, but venomous snakes are found on every continent except Antarctica. Here's what to do, and not to do, if you or a fellow human are bitten.

Do this:

☑ **Wash** the bite with soap and water.

☑ Keep the affected body part **immobile,** and lower than the heart if possible.

☑ Call for medical help, or go to a **hospital** as quickly as you can.

☑ If you cannot get medical care within 30 minutes, wrap a crêpe or elastic **bandage** 5-10cm (2–4in) above the bite to impede the flow of venom. But don't make it so tight as to cut off blood flow. (It should be loose enough to be able to slip a finger under it.)

☑ Take a **photo** of the snake if you can, or at least make some notes about its colour and size. This will help staff at the hospital identify it and administer the correct antivenin.

Don't do any of this:

☒ **Use ice** or hot packs.

☒ **Apply a tourniquet.**

☒ **Make incisions** of any kind to the wound.

☒ **Eat, drink or take medication.**

☒ **Apply mouth suction** to bite.
In addition, there's disagreement about the value of placing **suction cups** over the bite to draw out venom. Such devices are included in most commercially available snakebite kits, but many experts warn against using them.

☒ **Remove bandage** until in hospital.

☒ **Try to kill** the snake.

By the way, there's **no truth** in the idea that venomous snakes have slit, catlike pupils, while nonvenomous snakes have round pupils. Snakes have no eyelids, so to protect their eyes from bright lights (and when they are asleep), their pupils contract to a slit shape.

But, in the northeast USA (and only there), here's a colour rule to follow:

If **RED** touches **BLACK**, you're OK, Jack.

If **RED** touches YELLOW, you're a dead fellow.

(king snake)

(coral snake—deadly)

All snakes have forked tongues. Since they have poor eyesight and no ears, the tongue is a snake's primary sense organ, relaying airborne scents to the mouth. This results in a mixture of taste and smell.

DEADLY DOZEN

Stay out of their way.

(Actually, leave ALL snakes alone.)

Hook-nosed sea snake
Coastlines of S. Asia
Its venom is eight times more toxic than a cobra's.

Russell's viper
India

Inland taipan
Australia

Eastern brown
Australia

Black mamba
Africa
At 2.5m (8.2ft), it's one of the longest and fastest snakes. If a bite is not treated, the victim will probably die within 30 minutes.

Tiger rattlesnake
S.W. USA, N.W. Mexico

Boomslang
Africa

Blue krait
S.E. Asia, Indonesia
Its bite feels like a mosquito's, and it often strikes while the victim is asleep. They won't wake up ... ever.

Horned viper
Middle East, N. Africa

Tiger snake
Australia

Cobra
India
Medical upside: Alzheimer's researchers are looking at cobra venom as a possible therapy.

Puff adder
Africa

This list is based on *Snakes in Question*, by CH Ernst and GR Zug. Their 1996 paper ranked 80+ deadly snakes by the amount of their venom that's lethal to mice (called LD50). Snake venom works differently on different animals, including humans, but measuring the LD50 is the most common way to gauge a snake's venomosity.

Yoga on the road: the sun salutation

The sun salutation is a series of 12 poses performed in a single flow. It's often used as a warm-up routine before more vigorous poses. Even if you don't do any other yoga while you are travelling, do a couple of rounds of this; it's a good way to say hello to the day (even if there's no sun!).

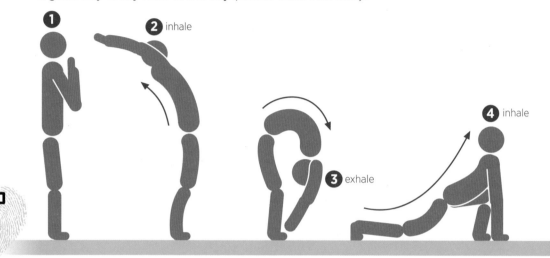

1

2 inhale

3 exhale

4 inhale

7 inhale

8 exhale

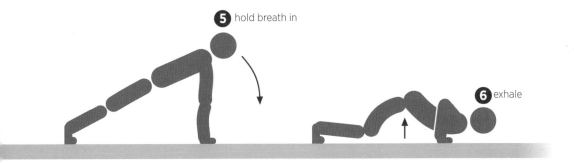

5 hold breath in

6 exhale

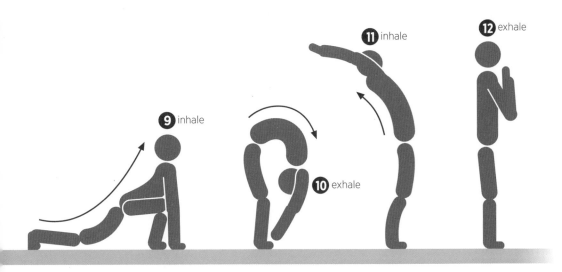

9 inhale

10 exhale

11 inhale

12 exhale

First aid

You might not be a doctor, but you can help yourself, and others.

A little history

- There are records from the 11th century showing that religious knights provided care to pilgrims, and trained other knights to treat battlefield injuries.

- In 1863, four nations met in Geneva to form what has become the Red Cross. Initially the organisation's aim was to treat wounded soldiers on the battlefield.

- In the USA, the Civil War (1861–65) prompted Clara Barton to organise the American Red Cross.

- The term "first aid" was coined in England in 1878, at the same time that civilians were taught first aid.

- Today there are first aid training organisations in many countries including Australia, Canada, Ireland, Singapore and the Netherlands.

Simple principles

Preserve life
Prevent further harm
Promote recovery

All sounds good to me. Let's go ...

Nosebleeds

1. Sit; lean forward slowly; keep the mouth open.

2. **Pinch the lower part of the nostril; hold for 15 minutes.** (Victim breathes through the mouth.)

3. Release slowly. Don't touch the nose, or blow it; you might start the bleeding again.

4. If bleeding has not stopped after 20 minutes, seek medical attention.

Hiccups

Most of the time, hiccups are **not medically significant.** Doctors dismiss the many folk remedies. But if your favourite cure works, go with it!

1. The most efficient "cures" concentrate on relaxing or stimulating the diaphragm; many of them feature odd ways of drinking water.

2. So **try this one:** stand up; take a sip of water; turn your head upside down and swallow slowly.

Minor burns

1. Remove watches, bracelets, rings or constricting clothing before the burned area begins to swell.

2. **Hold the burn under cold running water** for a few minutes.

3. Apply a cold compress* until the pain diminishes.

4. Dress the area with clean (if possible, sterile) nonfluffy material.

Major burns

1. **If clothes are on fire, douse the victim with water.**

2. **Wrap the injured person in a blanket;** place him or her on the ground. Do not try to remove clothing that is stuck to wounds.

3. **Cover exposed burned areas** with clean, dry nonfluffy material to stop infection; secure with a bandage.

4. **DO NOT:**
   - use adhesive dressings
   - apply butter or oil
   - apply lotions or creams
   - prick burn blisters
   - use fluffy materials

Motion sickness

It's caused by constant movement of the organ of balance in the inner ear, and also by the anxiety produced by previous attacks.

1 Various drugs are available to prevent or control motion sickness. **Antihistamines** help if taken about an hour before the start of a journey.

2 **Tip:** tell sufferers to focus on a point on the horizon rather than on nearby objects.

Blisters

1 They are best left to heal by themselves.

2 **Do not prick or burst blisters,** because the underlying tissue could become infected.

(The fluid inside a blister is a serum that has leaked from blood in the skin underneath after a minor injury, such as that caused by a tight-fitting shoe. The serum is sterile, and provides protection to the damaged tissue.)

Sunburn

1 Apply **calamine lotion** or sunburn cream.

2 Protect burned skin from further exposure.

3 Take analgesics (painkillers) to relieve tenderness.

4 Extreme burning may require a cream containing corticosteroid drugs prescribed by a doctor.

Heat stroke

Heat stroke differs from heat exhaustion (where the victim sweats profusely) in that sweating stops completely, the body becomes dry and flushed, and breathing is shallow.

1 **Seek medical help immediately.**

2 Move the victim to a cool shady place; remove clothing. Place the victim in a sitting position, leaning back slightly.

3 Cover with a wet sheet and keep it wet.

4 Fan with a magazine (or other suitable object) until their temperature drops to a normal range.

WHAT TO KEEP IN YOUR FIRST AID KIT

Just pack **necessities**— your kit must be portable.
- adhesive tape
- antiseptic cream
- antiseptic wipes
- aspirin
- bandages:
    absorbent gauze
    adhesive
    elastic
- calamine lotion
- foil or "space" blanket
- roll of sterile cotton
- rubbing alcohol
- safety pins
- scissors
- torch (check batteries!)
- tweezers

If possible, include a **mobile phone** (cellphone) in your kit. (Put an old one in there. It still needs a battery to turn it on, but even if your contract has expired, the emergency number for the country you are travelling in should still work.)

*A **cold compress** is a pad of material soaked in ice-cold water and held in place with a bandage. It reduces pain and swelling. (A compress that has been soaked in hot water increases the circulation and is useful for bringing boils to a head. A dry compress is used to stop bleeding from a wound.)

More first aid

Additional ways you can help in emergencies.

Diarrhoea

This is usually caused by food poisoning.

1 **To prevent dehydration,** dissolve 1 teaspoon of salt and 4 teaspoons of sugar in 9.5L (1qt) of water; drink 0.5L (1pt) of the mixture every hour.

2 Don't eat any solid food until the diarrhoea subsides.

3 If the condition persists for more than a week, or if there's blood visible, you should go to a doctor.

Removing a splinter

1 **Don't apply pressure or try squeezing to get it out.** (You might embed it further.)

2 Wash the area with soap and water. Pat dry; don't let the skin get soggy.

3 Inspect carefully: the angle the splinter entered will be its best route out!

There are several ways to remove splinters. Here are two interesting noninvasive methods.

Using baking soda:

1 Make a paste with a small amount of baking soda and water.

2 Put the mixture on a bandage and apply it to the affected area.

3 Leave it on for 24 hours, then remove.

4 The splinter should be sticking out of the skin, and should be easily removed with tweezers.

5 If necessary, repeat with new paste.

Using a potato:

1 Cut a potato into slices.

2 Place a slice on the affected area.

3 Hold it there, but don't apply pressure.

4 The potato should draw the splinter right out.

5 Optional celebration of successful splinter removal: put the rest of the potato on a skewer and cook it over the campfire.

Using a splint for a broken leg

Splints are used to prevent movement of a fractured limb. An improvised splint can be made from a piece of wood or a rolled-up magazine or newspaper.

1 If help is on the way, do not move the victim, but support the leg by putting one hand above the break, the other below it.

2 If the ambulance or other help is delayed, put a soft cloth around the splint then place it between the victim's knees and ankles.

3 Gently bring the uninjured leg toward the injured one.

4 Tie the ankles and feet together with a bandage in a figure-of-eight formation, secured on the uninjured side.

5 Tie bandages around the knees and thighs, avoiding the fracture site. All knots should be tied on the uninjured side.

6 Wait for help to arrive.

Sprained ankle

1 Make the victim as comfortable as possible.

2 **Apply a cold compress** (see "First Aid" spread) to the ankle; leave it on for 30 minutes.

3 Firmly bandage the lower leg and ankle (but not the toes) in a figure-of-eight formation.

4 Seek medical help. An x-ray may be needed.

Stings

1 Plants such as **nettles** carry tiny amounts of liquid that can irritate, but the effect wears off after an hour or so. Calamine lotion will soothe the irritation.

2 For a **jellyfish sting,** apply vinegar to inactivate the stinging liquid. Scrape off any fragments of tentacle; take an analgesic painkiller.

3 For a **scorpion bite,** take painkillers and apply a cold compress. (In some cases, antivenin may need to be given intravenously.)

Removing a fish hook

1 **If the hook is large or deeply embedded, go to a doctor at once.**

2 If it's a small hook, do not try to withdraw it the way it went in. Instead, **cut off the end of the hook** (including the circular loop that's attached to the fishing line), so that just a shaft of metal is left.

3 Swab the hook and surrounding area with rubbing alcohol.

4 Force the point of the hook forwards and up through the skin until it can be pulled out, making a **second puncture** in the skin.

5 Put some antibacterial cream and a bandage on the wounds.

There are other methods of removing fish hooks, but one way to avoid the problem altogether is to **use barbless hooks.** It's more fish-friendly if you are going to release the fish, and for you it's a painless way to get rid of a hook if you are caught by one.

Bleeding

1 Before tending to a victim's wound, **wash your hands** with soap and water if possible.

2 If a cut has dirt in it, rinse it under lukewarm water.

3 With a sterile gauze, dab the cut gently to dry it.

4 Cover with an adhesive bandage.

If it's a deep cut:

1 Raise the injured part and support it.

2 **Put a sterile dressing on the wound; apply firm pressure.**

3 If blood seeps through, don't remove the blood-soaked dressing (that might disturb clots and restart bleeding).

4 Put more dressings on top of the first one, and bandage them all together.

How to deliver a baby in an emergency

Remember this: most of the time, a baby delivers itself. Follow these pointers, though, and you'll make it easier for the mother.

If possible, have these things ready:

Two clean pieces of string, 22cm (9in) long, for tying the cord (shoelaces will do).

Sterilised scissors— boil them for 10 minutes and wrap them in a clean cloth.

Plastic bag for the afterbirth.

Soft blanket for the baby.

Container in case the mother vomits.

For some women, childbirth is a relatively painless experience. But others go through great pain. **Be prepared.**

1 **Wash your hands.**

2 You know the birth process is starting when muscles in the mother's uterus begin to contract at regular intervals. (If it's the mother's first baby, a good sign that the baby is nearly ready is when these **contractions are about 5 minutes apart and last from 40 to 90 seconds.)**

3 As the time between the contractions gets shorter, the mother feels them to be more intense. Her cervix dilates, and the mucus plug is discharged (her "water" breaks).

4 Contractions push the baby from the uterus to and through the vagina. As the baby emerges from the mother's body, **cradle the head but don't pull it.** The head usually comes out facing down, and returns to a normal position as the shoulders emerge (one at a time).

5 **Check if the umbilical cord is wrapped around the baby's neck.** If it is, slip it over the baby's head.

6 After the shoulders are out, the rest of the body should slide out easily with the next contraction.

7 **Wipe away any mucus** or blood from the baby's mouth.

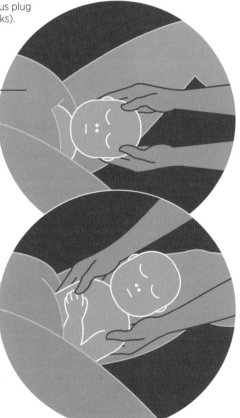

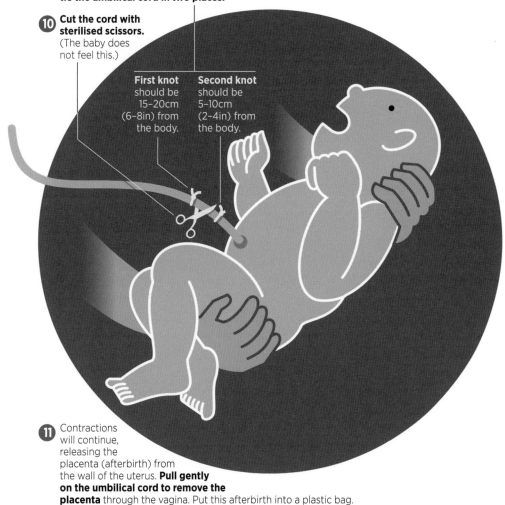

8 **Do not slap the baby on the back.** Instead, blow on the chest or tap the feet.

9 When the baby has been fully delivered, **tie the umbilical cord in two places.**

10 **Cut the cord with sterilised scissors.** (The baby does not feel this.)

First knot should be 15–20cm (6–8in) from the body.

Second knot should be 5–10cm (2–4in) from the body.

11 Contractions will continue, releasing the placenta (afterbirth) from the wall of the uterus. **Pull gently on the umbilical cord to remove the placenta** through the vagina. Put this afterbirth into a plastic bag.

How to perform a tracheotomy

This is serious stuff. You'd only slice someone's throat after trying all other ways—including the Heimlich manoeuvre—to restore their ability to breathe.

1 Ask someone to **call for medical help.**

2 Feel for the **slight dip between the Adam's apple and the cricoid cartilage.** That's where you are going to cut. Make a mark on the neck with a pen if you like.

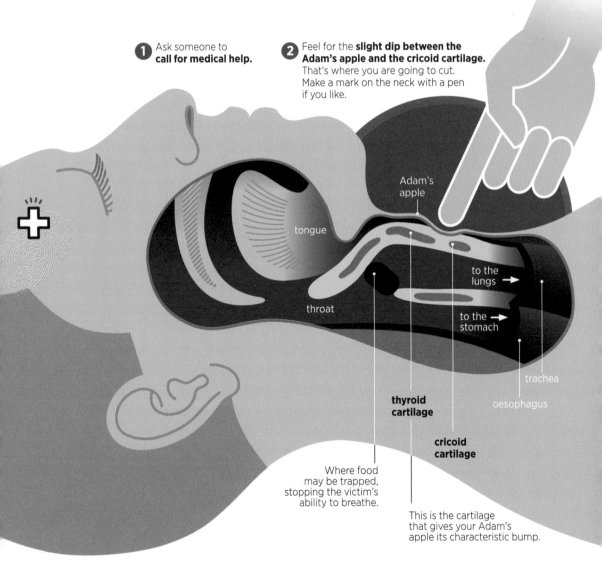

Adam's apple

tongue

to the lungs →

throat

to the → stomach

trachea

oesophagus

thyroid cartilage

cricoid cartilage

Where food may be trapped, stopping the victim's ability to breathe.

This is the cartilage that gives your Adam's apple its characteristic bump.

3 With a clean, sharp razor, **make a horizontal cut** about 1cm (0.4in) across and 1cm (0.4in) deep. There should not be too much blood.

4 Open the cut slightly with your finger and **insert a straw into the cut.** (The straw should be the biggest you have. If you have only thin ones, use two. Substitutes could be the barrel of a pen or a rolled up card.)

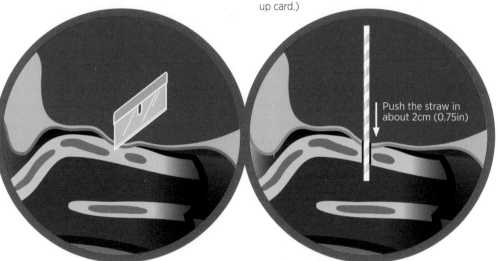

Push the straw in about 2cm (0.75in)

5 **Breathe into the straw quickly. Wait 5 seconds, then breathe again. Repeat once every 5 seconds.**

6 The whole process—from the failure of the Heimlich manoeuvre to the victim breathing on his or her own through the tube—must take **no longer than 3 minutes.** (3 minutes without oxygen means brain death.)

FOOD & DRINK

How to open a beer with a spoon

Don't worry if you can't find the bottle opener. Using a variety of everyday metal objects* (such as a spoon), the cap can easily be removed.

You can also do it with your teeth, but it's not recommended.

1 Grip the neck of the bottle firmly at the top, and put your thumb on the cap.

2 Resting the bowl of the spoon on your forefinger, hook the spoon under the cap.

the horse's mouth

pale ale

the horse's mouth

pale ale

* If there's no spoon around, you can also try these as levers to get the top off:

belt buckle
fork
car seatbelt latch
metal nail clippers
hammer
back of chef's knife

3 With your finger as a fulcrum, push down hard on the handle of the spoon to flip the cap off.

Surprisingly, it won't hurt.

4 If it doesn't work on the first attempt, just keep moving the spoon around the cap and repeat the downward pressure on the handle until the cap is loosened enough to come off.

Pretty soon, you'll be drinking.

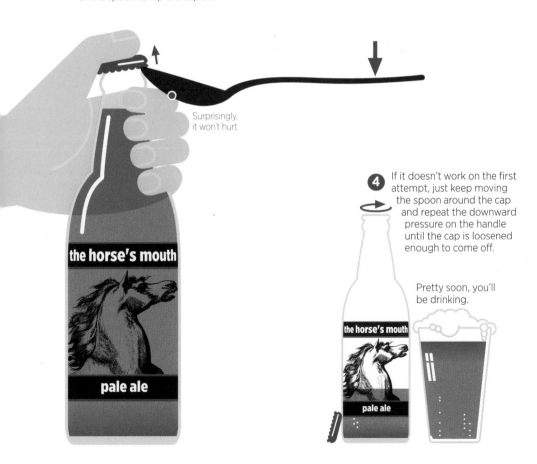

the horse's mouth

pale ale

How to open a coconut
Smash it or tap it?

Brute force

1 There are **three dark indentations** at the blunt end of a coconut: two "eyes" and a "mouth", forming a triangle. They are the weakest parts of the outer shell.

2 **Nestle** the coconut into a folded TOwEL.

3 Drive a strong, sharp object, such as a nail or screwdriver, into **two** of the holes (one is to let air in). Wiggle the objects a bit and remove.

4 Turn the coconut over and place on a glass to **drain** the coconut water.

The clear liquid is a popular drink in the tropics. Recent marketing claims for its health benefits are mostly unfounded.

5 Put the coconut in a plastic bag, and **whack** it.

6 You can keep the bits in the fridge for up to 7 days, or in the freezer for 3 months.

A gentler approach

1 With the coconut in your hand, use the back of a kitchen knife to **tap** the edge of the coconut around **its "equator".**

2 **Rotate** as you tap. Eventually it will split into two pieces. You might lose some of the water.

(If you don't have a knife handy, try tapping the coconut on the edge of a brick or rock.)

Optional (if you are at home, not on the beach)

3 Here's a way to loosen the flesh inside. Before doing the tapping, **bake** the coconut (at 93°C/200°F) for 15 minutes. Or put it in the **freezer** for 15 minutes.

If you do this, the inner husk will easily come away from the outer husk once it's opened.

4 The best way to remove the inner husk is to use a **potato peeler.**

And if you are in the jungle

5 Since you might not have any tools available, this could be a good way to open it.

Impale the blunt end of the coconut onto a strong, sharp stick.

Nice and shady but potentially dangerous.

How do you say Cheers! in China?

A phonetic pronunciation guide
to toasting around the world.

Albania 🥂 *geh-zoo-ah*

Armenia (West) 🥂 *genatzt*

Bosnia and Herzegovinia 🥂 *zhee-vi-lee*

Bulgaria 🥂 *naz-dra-vey*

Myanmar (Burma) 🥂 *au-ng my-in par say*

China (Mandarin) 🥂 *gan bay*

Croatia 🥂 *zhee-ve-lee / naz-dra-vlee*

Czech Republic 🥂 *naz-drah vi*

Denmark 🥂 *skoal*

Egypt 🥂 *fe sahetek*

England 🥂 *cheers*

Estonia 🥂 *ter-vih-sex*

Finland 🥂 *kippis*

France 🥂 *ah vot-re sahn-tay*

Germany 🥂 *prost*

Greece 🥂 *yamas*

Guam (Chamorro) 🥂 *bih-bah*

Hawaii 🥂 *okole maluna*

Hungary 🥂 *eggesh ay-ged-reh*

Iceland 🥂 *sk-owl*

Ireland (Gaelic) 🥂 *slawn-cha*

Israel 🥂 *l'chaim*

It's thought that touching glasses
started as a way to make sure the drinks
were not poisoned. (One drink might spill over
into the other.) Another story suggests that the word
toast is connected to a 17th-century French custom of
flavouring drinks with spiced toast. Or perhaps a long
forgotten Henry Toast named the custom after himself.

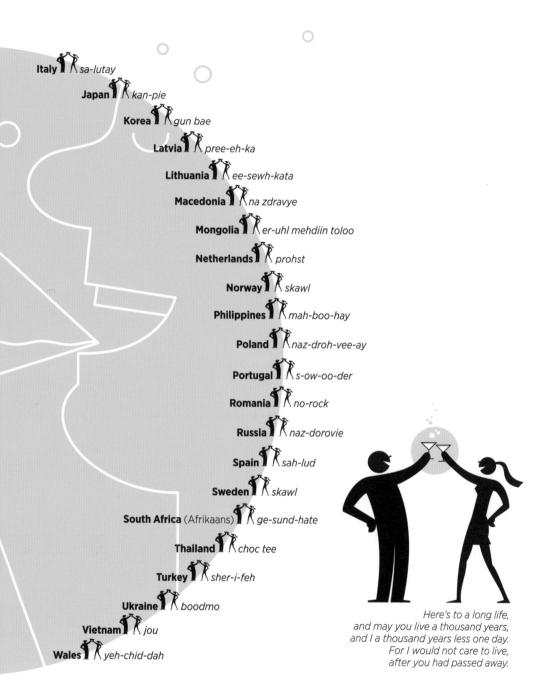

Italy 𝙃 sa-lutay

Japan 𝙃 kan-pie

Korea 𝙃 gun bae

Latvia 𝙃 pree-eh-ka

Lithuania 𝙃 ee-sewh-kata

Macedonia 𝙃 na zdravye

Mongolia 𝙃 er-uhl mehdiin toloo

Netherlands 𝙃 prohst

Norway 𝙃 skawl

Philippines 𝙃 mah-boo-hay

Poland 𝙃 naz-droh-vee-ay

Portugal 𝙃 s-ow-oo-der

Romania 𝙃 no-rock

Russia 𝙃 naz-dorovie

Spain 𝙃 sah-lud

Sweden 𝙃 skawl

South Africa (Afrikaans) 𝙃 ge-sund-hate

Thailand 𝙃 choc tee

Turkey 𝙃 sher-i-feh

Ukraine 𝙃 boodmo

Vietnam 𝙃 jou

Wales 𝙃 yeh-chid-dah

*Here's to a long life,
and may you live a thousand years,
and I a thousand years less one day.
For I would not care to live,
after you had passed away.*

Drink up!

Here are a few ideas about how the word "cocktail" came about:

● It was the custom to put a feather (from a cock's tail) into the drink to alert non-drinkers that it contained alcohol.

● It's derived from the French word *"coquetier"*. A coquetier was an eggcup used in New Orleans in the 19th century to serve certain drinks.

● It's derived from the Latin *aqua decocta* meaning distilled water.

● Since cocktails were once a morning drink, it's a metaphor for the rooster waking us up.

● Colonial taverns in the USA used to keep spirits of all kinds in wooden casks, and as the level of the liquid went down, the spirits lost some of their flavour and potency. The inn-keeper poured the "tailings" from different casks into one from which he could sell drinks at a reduced price to boozers who asked for "cock tailings".

I don't care. You? *Not now I have a martini.*

Doing shots

To keep things simple, all the ingredients in the drinks shown here are measured in shots. (Sounds a bit odd for juices, etc, but it's easier to keep the measures all the same.)

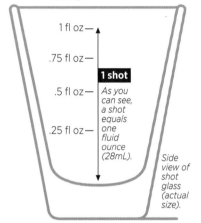

1 fl oz —
.75 fl oz —
1 shot
.5 fl oz — *As you can see, a shot equals one fluid ounce (28mL).*
.25 fl oz —

Side view of shot glass (actual size).

What does "proof" mean?

Proof is the measurement of alcoholic strength. One degree of proof equals half a percent of alcohol, so if you've got a bottle that's 75 proof, it is 35% alcohol; if the bottle says 100 proof, it has 50% alcohol in it. (There are many kinds of alcohol, but only ethyl alcohol is in wine, beer and spirits.)

Wine ranges from 12% to 20% alcohol; lager beer is around 4% to 5%; a few beers go up to 9%. The wonderful Thomas Hardy's Ale is 11.7%, and I guess that's why it comes in small bottles. Cough suppressants can be as high as 25%.

Each of these makes one drink.

MARTINI
1.5 shots vodka or gin
dash dry vermouth
*Shaken in ice;
add olives on a stick.*
(Cocktail onions in gin make this a **Gibson.**)

COSMOPOLITAN
2 shots vodka
1 shot Cointreau
1 shot cranberry juice
juice of half a lime
Shaken in ice.

PINA COLADA
1 shot light rum
3 shots pineapple juice
1 shot coconut cream
soda water
*Put in blender with crushed ice; blend;
add cherries and pineapple cubes on a stick.*

CAIPIRINHA
1.5 shots cachaca
1 teaspoon sugar
half lime cut into wedges
4–5 mint leaves
Muddle lime, sugar and mint until lime is juiced and sugar liquefied; add cachaca; shake well in cocktail shaker; pour into a rocks glass with ice.

MOJITO
1.5 shots light rum
2 shots soda water
1 teaspoon sugar
half lime cut into wedges
4–5 mint leaves
*Muddle lime, sugar and mint in a tall glass filled with crushed ice;
add rum; top with soda water; stir well.*

WHISKY SOUR

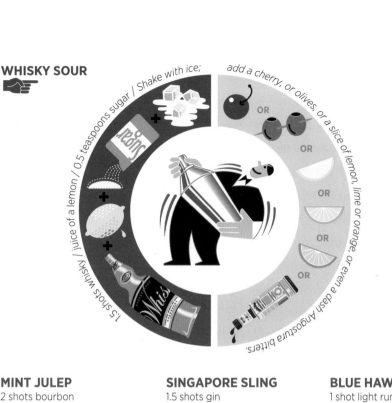

1.5 shots whisky / juice of a lemon / 0.5 teaspoons sugar / Shake with ice; add a cherry, or olives, or a slice of lemon, lime or orange, or even a dash Angostura bitters.

OR
OR
OR
OR
OR

The ingredients and quantities here are not set in stone. The amount of liquor in all cocktails can be varied to suit your taste: stronger, weaker or spicier.

MINT JULEP

2 shots bourbon
bunch of fresh mint
1 shot simple syrup*
Muddle 4–5 mint leaves with simple syrup in a glass; fill glass with crushed ice. Add bourbon, stir well; add more ice and stir again until ice forms on the outside of the glass. Push mint sprigs into the crushed ice so the top of the glass is entirely covered in mint.

*Simple syrup
Equal parts
water and sugar.
Heat the water until it simmers; add the sugar. Don't let the mixture boil, but stir until the sugar is completely dissolved. Remove from heat and allow to cool.

SINGAPORE SLING

1.5 shots gin
0.5 shot cherry liqueur
0.25 shot Cointreau
0.25 shot Bénédictine
0.25 shot grenadine
4 shots pineapple juice
1 shot lemon juice
dash Angostura bitters
Shaken in ice.

SIDECAR

1 shot Rémy Martin
0.5 shot Cointreau
1 lemon
sugar
Rim glass with lemon juice and sugar; put the glass in the freezer. Squeeze and strain lemon into a shaker; add liquor and ice; shake well; pour into frozen glass.

It's called a sidecar because you pour the balance of the mixture into a small glass placed beside the cocktail glass (for a refill).

BLUE HAWAIIAN

1 shot light rum
2 shots pineapple juice
1 shot blue curaçao
1 shot coconut cream
Blend with ice in tall glass; decorate with a pineapple slice and a cherry.

SCREWDRIVER

1.5 shots vodka
4.5 shots orange juice
With ice in tall glass.

BLOODY MARY

1.5 shots vodka
3 shots tomato juice
0.5 shot lemon juice
dash Worcestershire sauce
dash hot sauce
1 teaspoon horseradish
pinch salt & pepper
With ice in tall glass; add a celery stick.

Wine scents

Trying to describe the taste of wine is hard. In 1984, Professor Ann Noble of the University of California developed an **aroma wheel** and there are now many different wheels in use.* Here's a simplified linear version. Soon you'll be able to **join the wine snobs and talk like a pro!**

1

Most of what we think we are tasting in wine (and food) is actually what we can **smell.** In fact, our tongues have receptors for just **five** basic tastes, while our noses can distinguish between 4,000 and 10,000 aromas.

BITTER
UMAMI (eg meat, MSG)
SOUR
SALT
SWEET

2

In wine circles, **aroma** is the term applied to the smell that new wines acquire from their grapes.

Bouquet is technically the smell of the wine after it has developed and aged in the bottle. However, many people continue to use the term "aroma" after the bottle is opened (that's why the aroma wheel is called that).

*Google **aroma wheel** to see lots of examples of aroma charts and wheels.

3

Take a sip; does it taste...

Think about it; does it remind you of...

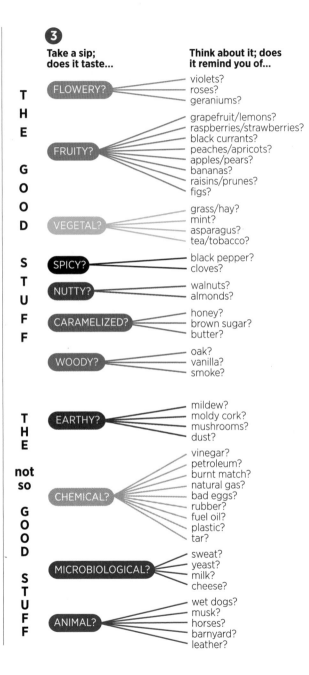

THE GOOD STUFF

FLOWERY?
- violets?
- roses?
- geraniums?

FRUITY?
- grapefruit/lemons?
- raspberries/strawberries?
- black currants?
- peaches/apricots?
- apples/pears?
- bananas?
- raisins/prunes?
- figs?

VEGETAL?
- grass/hay?
- mint?
- asparagus?
- tea/tobacco?

SPICY?
- black pepper?
- cloves?

NUTTY?
- walnuts?
- almonds?

CARAMELIZED?
- honey?
- brown sugar?
- butter?

WOODY?
- oak?
- vanilla?
- smoke?

THE not so GOOD STUFF

EARTHY?
- mildew?
- moldy cork?
- mushrooms?
- dust?

CHEMICAL?
- vinegar?
- petroleum?
- burnt match?
- natural gas?
- bad eggs?
- rubber?
- fuel oil?
- plastic?
- tar?

MICROBIOLOGICAL?
- sweat?
- yeast?
- milk?
- cheese?

ANIMAL?
- wet dogs?
- musk?
- horses?
- barnyard?
- leather?

4

Here's an amusing test you can try with your drinking buddies.

Is it **WHITE** or is it RED ?

First blindfold a couple of people. then give them a glass of red wine and ask if they can tell you if it's red or white. Then do the opposite, and give them a glass of white, and see if they know. You'll be surprised at the answers.

Next, out of sight of your friends, put two drops of red food colouring and one drop of blue food colouring into a full-bodied white wine (such as a chardonnay).

Take off the blindfolds and give the drinkers a glass of this mixture and then glass of red wine, and see if they can tell the difference. Many professional wine experts have failed both these tests.

Seasoned drinkers will soon catch on that it's the smell that's the most important way to tell the difference, but when we can *see* the colour it's amazing how much we are conditioned by what the wine looks like. Try it!

You know, we were making wine in Egypt about 5,000 years ago.

Really? Did you know that treading grapes is illegal in some parts of the USA nowadays?

How to prevent a hangover ...

Everyone has a pet way to do this.
Here's a collection of remedies. Take your pick.

BEFORE DRINKING

1 **Eat fried food;** it makes you absorb alcohol more slowly (though you will eventually absorb it all).

2 **Drink milk;** it lines the stomach.

WHILE DRINKING

1 **Drink water** between alcoholic drinks.

2 **Eat something** while you drink. OK, not exactly *while* you drink, that could be messy. (Or fun, depending on how the evening is going.)

The bad and the better
The old saying "beer before wine, you'll be fine" is cute, but the order in which you drink different things really doesn't make any difference. It's the *amount* you consume that makes you drunk.

This is the order of hangover-makingness:

BAD
Your hangover will probably be worse if you drink spirits that have a deep colour.

brandy
red wine
rum
whisky
white wine
gin
vodka
beer

BETTER

 water (designated driver)

or cure one

AT BEDTIME

1 Drink a lot of **water.**

2 Take **two Alka-Seltzer.**

3 **Close curtains,** or pull down blinds so room is dark in the morning.

Portrait of El Lissitzky with a hangover.

IN THE MORNING

(An old Irish custom: to cure a hangover, bury the ailing person up to the neck in moist sand.)

What you are feeling is the effects of dehydration, caused by alcohol.

DO this:

1 **Sleep longer,** if you have the time. (That's why you shut the light out.)

2 **Add a lemon slice** (for vitamin C) **to room-temperature water** and drink.

3 Drink **juice** for more vitamin C. (Tomato juice is good too.)

4 Eat plain, **burnt toast** (the carbon acts as a kind of filter); it boosts your blood sugar.

5 Eat **fruit** (bananas are good), a bacon sandwich, any mineral-rich food, such as pickles or canned fish.

6 **Take aspirin or ibuprofen** (note "don'ts" below).

7 **Shower.** Sounds obvious, but works wonders.

8 Go for a **walk.**

DON'T try any of these:

1 **Hair of the dog.** Many swear by the idea that a little more of what you had the night before will solve your problem. It might disguise your aching head a little, but it won't help cure it!

2 **Paracetamol-based pills** (these put even more strain on your liver and kidney).

3 **Hangover pills;** few work. And diet sodas or soft drinks don't help.

4 **Coffee:** it'll dehydrate you more.

5 **Any dairy products:** they'll make you feel more queasy.

☕ We love coffee ...

The world consumes **2.3 billion cups a day,** and there are many ways to drink it. For instance, here are six of the many **espresso** variations:

carajillo	cortado	doppio	guillermo	macchiato	ristretto
espresso + brandy	espresso + milk	double espresso	espresso + lime	espresso + foamed milk	espresso + less water

☕ How much?

These average prices for a **regular cup of coffee** are from a recent survey. Prices vary, of course, according to world market fluctuations and crop shortages, among other factors.

MOSCOW	$10.20
PARIS	$6.80
ATHENS	$6.60
BEIJING	$6.28
BERLIN	$5.20
TOKYO	$5.05
NEW YORK CITY	$3.80
JOHANNESBURG	$2.40
BUENOS AIRES	$2.00
SEOUL	50¢

All prices are US$.

☕ A very short history

The **Chinese discovered the effects of caffeine,** in the form of medicinal tea, about **5,000 years ago.** Coffee was introduced to Europe at the beginning of the 1600s. By the early 1700s, **Bach** had written his "Coffee Cantata" operetta while intellectuals such as Voltaire and Rousseau, frequenters of Paris's many coffee houses, praised the drink's ability to keep them "Enlightened".

and *why* we love it: caffeine!

☕ What is caffeine?

It's a stimulant found in more than 60 plants, including coffee beans and tea leaves. In its pure form, it's a white, bitter-tasting crystalline powder. The chemical structure, first identified in 1819, is nearly identical to that of **adenosine,** a chemical in the brain that slows activity and helps to regulate sleep.

☕ How does it work?

Since the molecular structure of caffeine is very similar to that of adenosine, **caffeine "poses" as adenosine** in the flow of messages from one brain cell to the next.

1 When there's no caffeine present, adenosine (◐) can flow unrestricted from one brain cell to receptors on the adjoining cell.

end of one brain cell

receptor sites on next brain cell

2 But when caffeine (◐) is present, it fits perfectly into the receptors, fooling the brain cell and effectively suppressing the calming action of the adenosine.

3 With the adenosine blocked, more neurons start firing in the brain. This increased activity triggers the production of adrenaline, which causes your pupils to dilate, your heart to beat faster, and your blood pressure to rise. Your liver releases fatty acids and sugar into the bloodstream, giving you extra energy.

☕ How long does it stay in your system?

If you have a cup of coffee with 200mg of caffeine in it at 9am, there will still be 100mg of caffeine left in your body at 3pm.

200 mg   100 mg

How to roll a burrito

And what to put inside it before you do!

①

Put a **corn tortilla** on a plate and spread some **sour cream** in the middle of it.

②

Put some small pieces of cooked **chicken** onto the sour cream, and a dollop of **salsa*** on top of that.

Fold the bottom edge of the tortilla towards the centre.

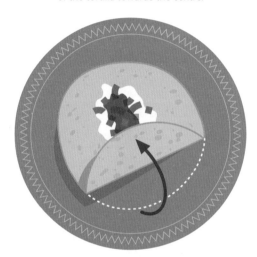

You can add **hot sauce** at any stage while you are making the burrito. But **beware,** there are some real mouth blasters out there. Try a drop before you go wild with the bottle.

For the chicken
You can make it easy for yourself if you use already-cooked chicken chopped into small chunks.

Put the chunks into a saucepan, and add:
cumin, hot chilli powder, a little salt, paprika and minced garlic.

Toss the chicken with the spicy mix to coat the pieces. Then add a little water to the pan and gently heat through.

3

Fold one side of the
tortilla into the centre.

4

Roll the whole thing
into a tube that's open
at one end.

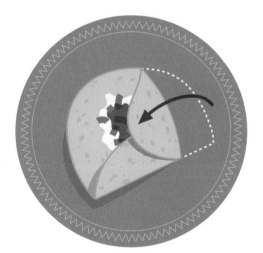

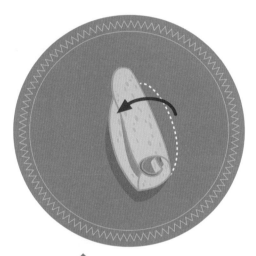

*For the salsa
Mix:
**chopped tomatoes,
coriander (cilantro) or
parsley, hot peppers
and onions, minced garlic
and oil.**

It doesn't matter if
you make
too much—it will
keep in the fridge for
a week or so.
(And it always seems
to get better
with age.)

EXTRA! Try adding some
guacamole at step **2**.

For that, mash together:
**chopped tomatoes, coriander (cilantro), onions
and ripe avocados, with a little lemon
or lime juice.**

If you chop the ingredients
really finely before mashing, you'll get
a smooth green guacamole. But if you
chop everything coarsely, and go light on
the mashing, you'll end up with a chunky mix.
Both are nice.

(This will keep for a couple of days in the
fridge. It will turn a rather unattractive
brown, but it's OK to eat.)

Want a thrill? Eat fugu. Carefully!

The fish

● The **fugu** (from two Chinese characters meaning "river" and "pig") is also known as the pufferfish, blowfish or globefish, because it can puff itself up with water, to make it look bigger to its enemies in the sea.

● However, the fugu hardly needs to do the blowing up thing, because the fish also contains a **deadly poison**—another natural defence mechanism to ward off predators.

● The poison, **tetrododoxin,** is found in the skin, skeleton, ovaries, intestines and particularly the liver.

The food

● Fugu has long been a delicacy in Japan, and there are about 3,800 fugu restaurants in the country today.

● Preparation is strictly controlled by law; fugu chefs must go through rigorous training for years to gain the certification that allows them to prepare the fish for human consumption. At the end of the training, there is a test in which the chef must prepare a fugu dish—and eat it!

● In restaurants, fugu is usually eaten raw, as sashimi, cut into very thin slices. Opinion is mixed about the taste; some say it's a bit like chicken, but it does have a delicate, gelatinous texture.

● If you want to order it yourself, make sure you see the chef's certificate before you commit! And if you aren't squeamish, read on to the next page.

The discarded organs and bones are placed in tightly sealed containers and taken away to be burned.

In Japan, the best time to eat fugu is in January and February.

There is evidence that the Egyptians knew about fugu poisoning. And the explorer James Cook described what some believe to be the deadly effect in his 1774 journal, aftersome crew members ate the fish.

The belly is covered with thousands of sharp, spiny quills.

The poison

● **If the fish is prepared properly, the flesh can be eaten safely.** It's even possible to eat parts of the organs if they are thoroughly washed out. Nevertheless, in Japan the most lethal part, the liver, cannot be sold, and the whole fish is banned in the European Union.

● Some people like to eat the fish with a tiny amount of toxin left in it. They feel a **tingling in the lips,** and it's this effect that attracts people. But it's a dangerous move, because if there is too much toxin, diners will soon experience something much worse.

● Tetrododoxin does not cross the blood-brain barrier, so the **victims remain fully conscious while their central nervous system gradually shuts down,** first producing dizziness and incoherent speech, then paralysing the muscles. This can lead to asphyxia, and possibly death. (There is no antidote for fugu poisoning.)

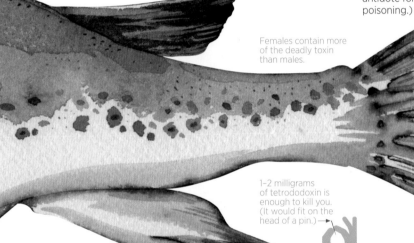

Females contain more of the deadly toxin than males.

1–2 milligrams of tetrododoxin is enough to kill you. (It would fit on the head of a pin.) →

And ...

● By restricting the fish's diet, some food companies are producing a **poison-free fugu** in aqua farms.

● As well as in Japanese restaurants, there are **other countries where you can eat fugu,** including the USA, and South Korea. (The fish itself is found in waters around the world.) The thrill of eating something that might kill you is clearly addictive.

● If you'd like a slightly **creepy Japanese souvenir,** lanterns are made from the cleaned skin of the fugu. You can also buy fugu-skin toys and waterproof wallets.

How to eat a lobster

It's messy. But plunge ahead anyway.

PINCHER CLAW

1 **Twist off the claws.**

2 **Crack each claw** with a nutcracker, pliers or hammer (or even a lobster claw cracker, if you have such a thing).

Although their eyes are prominent, lobsters are practically blind. But their short antennules sense distant odours carried by seawater, which helps them to find food, choose mates and decide if danger is near. The longer antennae are also sense organs.

EYE

ANTENNULES

EYE

ANTENNA

CRUSHER CLAW

What do lobsters eat?

Mostly they eat other animals: crabs, mussels, clams, starfish, sea urchins and shrimp. They also eat parts of their old shells after moulting. (The calcium strengthens the new shell that's forming.)

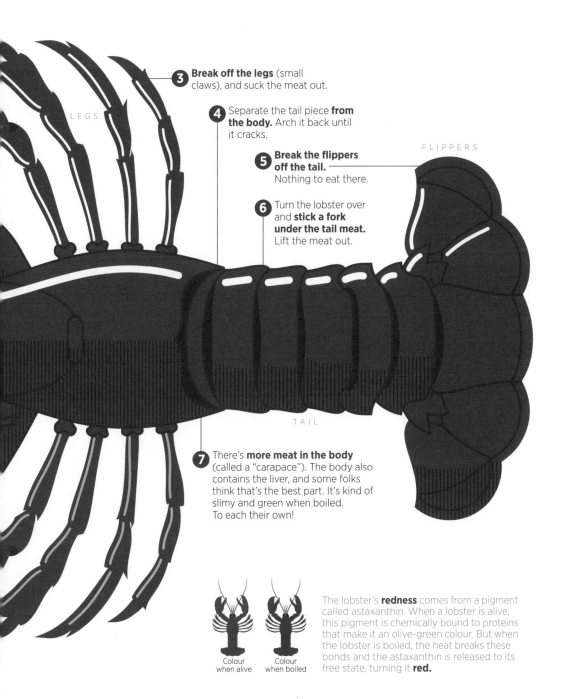

3 **Break off the legs** (small claws), and suck the meat out.

LEGS

4 Separate the tail piece **from the body.** Arch it back until it cracks.

FLIPPERS

5 **Break the flippers off the tail.** Nothing to eat there.

6 Turn the lobster over and **stick a fork under the tail meat.** Lift the meat out.

TAIL

7 There's **more meat in the body** (called a "carapace"). The body also contains the liver, and some folks think that's the best part. It's kind of slimy and green when boiled. To each their own!

Colour when alive

Colour when boiled

The lobster's **redness** comes from a pigment called astaxanthin. When a lobster is alive, this pigment is chemically bound to proteins that make it an olive-green colour. But when the lobster is boiled, the heat breaks these bonds and the astaxanthin is released to its free state, turning it **red.**

What to eat in the jungle

Some cultures eat insects and small animals as part of their daily diet; for others they are just a delicacy. For you, they might be all you can find.

Entomophagy is the word used by people who know about these things when they are talking about humans eating insects. (Animals that eat insects are called **insectivores.**)

You won't care about long words if you are hungry in the jungle or the bush, and you'll probably eat anything you can get your hands on.

Here are some dishes for your evening meal when you've run out of normal food.

Termites

You'll need to gather a great many of these tiny insects to make a meal. Some say they taste like peanut butter, others liken the taste to 10-day old curdled milk. But they are a good source of protein.

Frogs

This is the European edible frog (the kind French restaurants use when they serve frogs' legs), but there are many other frogs that you can eat. Skin all frogs before you cook them.

Beetle grubs

The white grubs of wood-infesting beetles are perfectly edible if you split their bodies and toast or fry them. You'll find them in decaying and rotten wood.

Birds

All birds are edible, but stay away from those that eat dead animals—vultures and kites—their flesh tastes terrible.

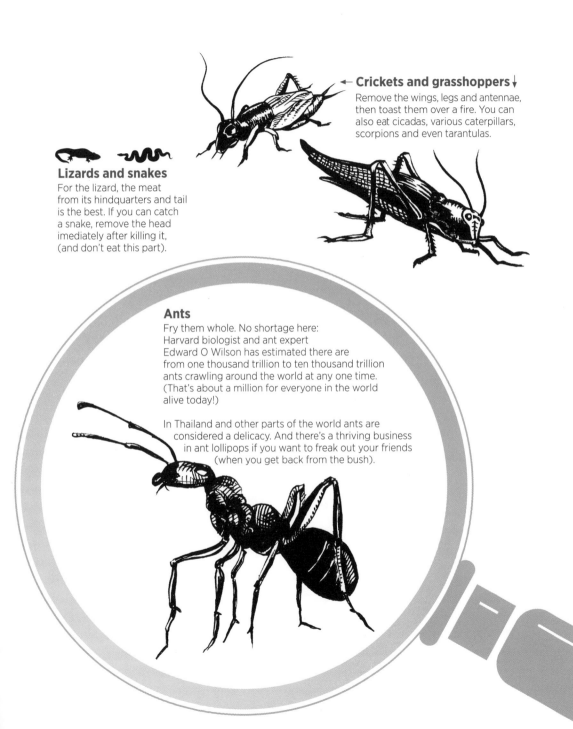

Crickets and grasshoppers ↓
Remove the wings, legs and antennae, then toast them over a fire. You can also eat cicadas, various caterpillars, scorpions and even tarantulas.

Lizards and snakes
For the lizard, the meat from its hindquarters and tail is the best. If you can catch a snake, remove the head imediately after killing it, (and don't eat this part).

Ants
Fry them whole. No shortage here: Harvard biologist and ant expert Edward O Wilson has estimated there are from one thousand trillion to ten thousand trillion ants crawling around the world at any one time. (That's about a million for everyone in the world alive today!)

In Thailand and other parts of the world ants are considered a delicacy. And there's a thriving business in ant lollipops if you want to freak out your friends (when you get back from the bush).

Travel is like a box of chocolates ... you never know what you're gonna get

Well, that's not exactly what Tom Hanks said in the film *Forrest Gump,* but here's lots of stuff about that box of chocolates you are taking home as a present for Mum.

Chocolate milestones

500 Cocoa powder was in use by the Mayans (traces have been found in their pottery).

1502 On his fourth voyage to the Americas, Columbus found a stash of cocoa beans in what is now Honduras and sent some back to the King of Spain. Beans were used as currency by the Aztecs.

1525 Conquistador Hernando Cortez introduced cocoa to Charles V of Spain. The Aztecs mixed powdered beans with chili peppers to make a bitter **chocolate drink;** Europeans discovered they could add sugar and vanilla instead.

1756 The first chocolate factory is opened in Germany.

1828 In Holland, Conrad van Houten patented a hydraulic press that squeezed much of the fat from roasted beans, leaving a substance that could be ground into a fine powder—**cocoa.**

1849 In England, Joseph Fry produced the first solid **eating chocolate.**

1879 In Switzerland, Daniel Peter mixed cocoa powder with powdered milk (invented by Swiss chemist Henri Nestle) to make **milk chocolate.**

1907 Milton Hershey produced his first *Kisses.*

1937 The English company Rowntree introduced *Chocolate Niblet Beans.* In 1938, they were renamed *Smarties.* (In the USA, Forrest Mars Sr. copied this idea, in 1941, calling his product *M&Ms.*)

2003 Kathryn Ratcliffe ate 138 *Smarties* in 3 minutes using chopsticks, and entered the *Guinness Book of Records.*

How it's made

1 The cacao beans are taken out of the pods and left to **ferment,** reducing their bitterness.

2 The beans are **dried, cleaned, graded** and **shipped** to chocolate processing plants, where they are **roasted.**

3 The hard outer shells are removed, leaving kernels (called **nibs**).

4 A machine with revolving heated granite rollers (called a "melangeur") **mashes** the nibs into a thick paste, called "chocolate liquor".

The melangeur

Chocolate liquor is the base from which all chocolate products are made.

5 The paste is heated to ensure a smooth consistency, in a process known as **conching.**

6 The liquid chocolate is alternately heated and cooled for several hours. This **tempering** gives the final product its sheen and the familiar crack when you break it apart.

7 The liquid is **moulded** and **cooled** (to harden it), and then finally **packaged.**

Top cocoa-producing countries
millions of metric tons

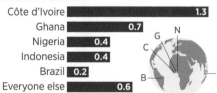

Country	millions of metric tons
Côte d'Ivoire	1.3
Ghana	0.7
Nigeria	0.4
Indonesia	0.4
Brazil	0.2
Everyone else	0.6

Where does the word "chocolate" come from?

Experts disagree, but it's probably from the Nahuatl* word *xocolatl*, which means "bitter water".

*A language indigenous to Central Mexico.

Spotty?

Academic institutions have done studies showing that eating chocolate does not cause acne.

Eating chocolate   Not eating chocolate

(Apparently the milk in milk chocolate has something to do with acne.)

Botany

The small cacao tree (*Theobroma cacao**) was originally found in the forests of Central and South America. It now grows in many countries 20 degrees above and below the equator.

The fruit of the cacao tree is a huge berry (or pod)—this is life-sized—that sprouts straight out of the branches and trunk of the tree.

There are 30 to 40 cacao beans inside each pod. It takes 10 pods to make 0.5kg (1lb) of cocoa.

*Named by Carl von Linné, an 18th-century Swedish scientist. *Theobroma* means "food of the gods".

PERSONAL SAFETY

How to defend yourself

Arguing in Istanbul? Someone insulting your girlfriend in Berlin? Here's hoping you don't have to fight over it, but just in case, here are three ways to get out of a sticky situation. (Hint: wear all blue, he's the winner here.)

Making your hotel room burglar proof

Some ways to stop yourself being an easy target for thieves.

1 BEFORE YOU GO ON A TRIP

- **Make a list** of your valuables, including models and serial numbers. You could take photos of them too. (Leave a copy of this at home—you don't want your list to get stolen!)

- Consider **insuring** your valuables.

- In case you are robbed, it's a good idea to have **copies of all your important documents** (air tickets, passport, visas etc); keep one set in a separate spot to the originals, and give another copy to someone at home.

2 WHEN YOU ARRIVE AT THE HOTEL

- When choosing your room, make sure the **entrance is well lit.** You may want to check if the hotel has security cameras. (Remember, travellers make great targets for thieves. You don't yet know your way around, or even who should be around.)

3 WHENEVER YOU LEAVE YOUR ROOM

- **Leave the lights on.** You could leave the TV or the radio on too.

- **Close the blinds** so no one can see what's inside or if anyone is there.

- Don't forget to **lock the doors** and close the windows! (And the balcony door if you're lucky enough to have a balcony.)

- If you've got a **"Do not disturb"** sign then hang it on your door so that thieves will think the room is occupied.

- If there's a telephone in the room, **turn down the ringer** so that no one can hear it ring out.

- **Pack your belongings back into your suitcase** before you leave your room; lock it if you have a lock. If someone enters your room and there's nothing on display they may not bother to look for anything.

- **Don't return your key to the front desk** on leaving your hotel if the key and room number will be hanging behind the desk, visible to everyone. (And announcing that you're not in there!)

- Protect your valuables. **Don't leave any cash, jewellery or your passport in your room.** If you must, then make it hard for them to be found—don't leave them out in the open. Thieves will want to get in and out quickly.

- If the hotel has a **safe,** consider putting your valuables in it.

- If you need to leave your valuables, consider hiding them by using tape to **fasten them to the underside of a wardrobe** or another piece of furniture.

- **If you see anyone suspicious, let reception know.**

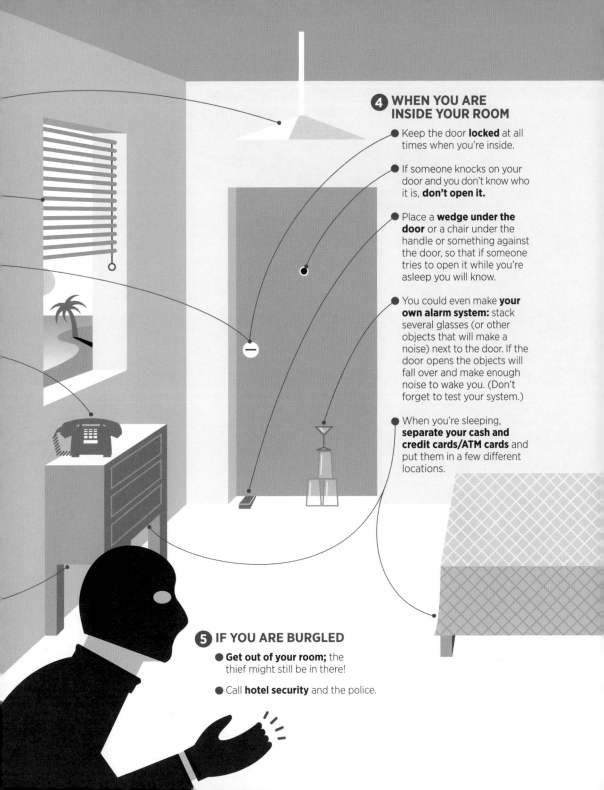

④ WHEN YOU ARE INSIDE YOUR ROOM

- Keep the door **locked** at all times when you're inside.

- If someone knocks on your door and you don't know who it is, **don't open it.**

- Place a **wedge under the door** or a chair under the handle or something against the door, so that if someone tries to open it while you're asleep you will know.

- You could even make **your own alarm system:** stack several glasses (or other objects that will make a noise) next to the door. If the door opens the objects will fall over and make enough noise to wake you. (Don't forget to test your system.)

- When you're sleeping, **separate your cash and credit cards/ATM cards** and put them in a few different locations.

⑤ IF YOU ARE BURGLED

- **Get out of your room;** the thief might still be in there!

- Call **hotel security** and the police.

Why must I turn off my mobile phone?

Read on; here's why!

● Most disputes among airline staff and passengers on planes are connected to the use of electronic devices. Many people refuse to turn off their mobile phones (or think it does not matter whether they don't). Since pilots now use iPads instead of bulky manuals, **what's the problem** for the rest of us?

● Airline security agencies say they cannot test the huge variety of electronic gadgets that we bring on board, and what the effect is if all of them are turned on at once.

● Crews have occasionally reported static on radio frequencies and false readings on landing systems. Attempts to recreate problems in laboratory settings have so far failed, but since there is the chance, however slight, that using your gadget might interfere with the plane's electronic systems, why not do as you are told, and **TURN IT OFF!**

(By the way, even if you are sitting far away from the cockpit, you may still be near an antenna, so don't think that makes you a special exception.)

● In the US, federal law can impose a fine or even jail time for this offence.

● You should **completely turn off your mobile phone** during the entire flight (don't just put it into flight mode) because when it is on it's connecting to many cell towers on the ground below, using up bandwidth. This could compromise the plane's communication systems.

It's for your own safety!

- Some airlines are planning to make cell connectivity available on board, but consumer groups opposed to noisy conversations are objecting.

- In the future, it is likely that **pico cells** will be installed inside aircraft. These cells will have the same function as small, ground-based cell towers, but the signals will not interfere with the plane's system. Quiet zones, or quiet times, may then have to be mandated to avoid a different kind of travel anger from less-wired passengers.

- **OK, so you turned it off.** (You do not have to disable heart pacemakers, hearing aids or portable voice recorders because their signals don't affect any of the plane's navigational systems.)

- But don't forget about your device and leave it on the plane. Airlines say they have hundreds of e-gadgets (iPads, tablet computers and e-readers) in their lost and found storage rooms.

- Before you travel:
  - Tape your business card to the back of all devices. (This helps airline staff in their search.)
  - Note your seat and flight numbers.
  - Keep serial numbers.
  - Supply your phone number when booking flights.
  - Enable any "Find my ..." features.

- If you do lose your device, don't forget to cancel any automatic subscriptions and credit card data associated with it before you replace it.

How to avoid being hit by lightning

Don't want to get fried? Read on.

1 When you hear thunder, you can be pretty sure that lightning will follow.

2 If the time between a flash of lightning and the sound of thunder is less than 30 seconds, (and you are outdoors) **move to a safe place.**

3 If you are anywhere above the treeline or in an open field, **MOVE!**

4 But if there's nowhere to go, **kneel with your hands on the ground.** Bow your head forward.

5 **DON'T stand near or go into any of these places:**

Safe places to go

● **Large enclosed buildings.** Once inside, avoid contact with showers, sinks, metal doors and window frames, as well as electrical outlets and cords, telephones and televisions—in fact anything that's wired.

● **Fully enclosed cars, trucks, buses and vans.** When you are inside, avoid contact with metal surfaces in these vehicles.

flagpoles
isolated trees
open shelters
metal seats and fences
lakes, rivers and oceans
swimming pools
convertibles
golf carts

What *is* lightning, anyway?

- Scientists are still debating the details of how lightning occurs, but it's an atmospheric electrical discharge—a spark—usually associated with cumulonimbus clouds (have a look at the page on clouds in this book).

- Lightning can travel at speeds up to 220,000km/h (140,000mph) and can reach a temperature of 30,000°C (54,000°F).

- There are 16 million lightning storms in the world each year.

- About 70% of lightning occurs in the tropics (where most thunderstorms happen).

- The most afflicted spot is the village of Kifuka, elevation 975m (3,200ft), in the Democratic Republic of the Congo. It receives an amazing 158 lightning strikes per square kilometre (0.39 square miles) a year.

6 While storms usually occur when it's dark (or at least cloudy), the danger from lightning can exist in sunshine, when the sky is clear.

How to drive in the snow

1 **PREPARE!**

❄ **Keep these items somewhere in the car:**
flashlight • jumper cables • nylon tow strap • energy bars • drinking water • shovel •
ice scraper • warm blanket • book or magazine to keep you occupied until help comes.

❄ **Brush away all snow.** When it blows off it might obstruct your view. The weight of snow on the roof of a car increases the car's stopping distance and alters its centre of gravity.

❄ **Clear ice and snow from the base of the windshield.** Wipers won't clog as quickly, and the vent there is often the fresh-air intake.

❄ **Keep fuel tank at least half full.** This keeps weight over the rear wheels. It also prevents condensation from forming in the tank and causing gas-line freezing.

❄ **Keep all headlights and rear lights clean.** You'll see and be seen.

3
**IF YOU
GET STUCK**

❄ **Don't spin the wheels.** Friction causes heat. A puddle of water will form under the wheels and turn to ice.

❄ **Dig snow out from under the car.** This will allow the wheels to rest firmly on the ground and gain traction.

❄ **If stranded, stay in the car.** It provides shelter and will be visible to rescuers. It's safe to run the engine for heat as long as you **keep the tailpipe area clear of snow.**

❄ **Put floor mats down for traction.**

② **DRIVE** (carefully!)

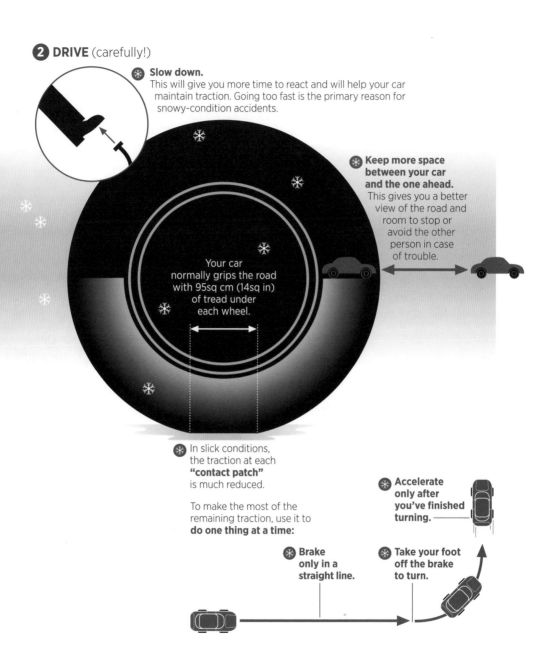

✳ **Slow down.**
This will give you more time to react and will help your car maintain traction. Going too fast is the primary reason for snowy-condition accidents.

✳ **Keep more space between your car and the one ahead.**
This gives you a better view of the road and room to stop or avoid the other person in case of trouble.

Your car normally grips the road with 95sq cm (14sq in) of tread under each wheel.

✳ In slick conditions, the traction at each **"contact patch"** is much reduced.

To make the most of the remaining traction, use it to **do one thing at a time:**

✳ **Accelerate only after you've finished turning.**

✳ **Brake only in a straight line.**

✳ **Take your foot off the brake to turn.**

OTHER FUN STUFF

Roadtrip! Let's go to weirdly named places!

Americans give their towns, cities and unincorporated communities the oddest, sexiest, silliest names. Some of them are slightly naughty, too, so if you're offended by that sort of thing, please turn the page.

OK, the rest of you, have a nice trip!

Where to next? Toad Suck, Arkansas?

All names guaranteed real. (You can't make this stuff up.)

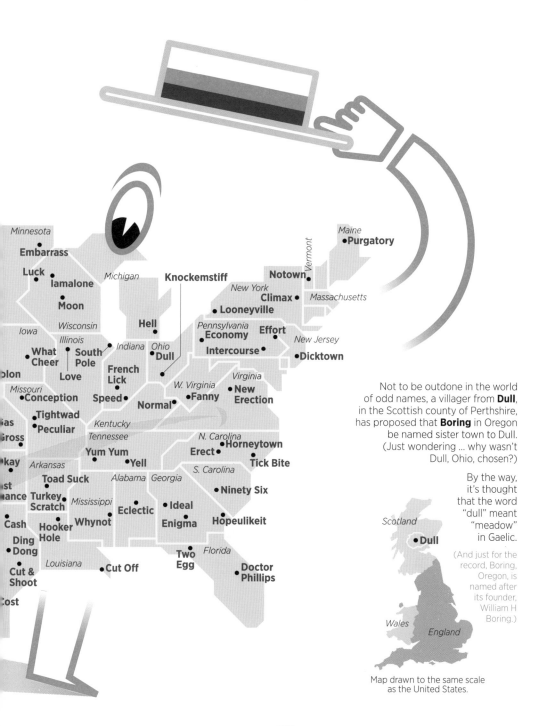

Minnesota

Embarrass

Luck
Iamalone

Michigan

Knockemstiff

Maine
Purgatory

Notown

Moon

New York

Climax

Massachusetts

Looneyville

Wisconsin

Hell

Pennsylvania

Effort

Iowa

Illinois

Indiana

Ohio

Economy

New Jersey

What
Cheer

South
Pole

Dull

Intercourse

Dicktown

lon

Love

French
Lick

Virginia

Missouri

Conception

Speed

W. Virginia

New
Erection

Fanny

Tightwad

Normal

as

Peculiar

Kentucky

ross

Tennessee

N. Carolina

Horneytown

Yum Yum

Erect

kay

Arkansas

Yell

S. Carolina

Tick Bite

Toad Suck

Alabama

Georgia

st
ance

Turkey
Scratch

Mississippi

Ninety Six

Eclectic

Ideal

Cash

Hooker
Hole

Whynot

Enigma

Hopeuliket

Ding

Dong

Louisiana

Two
Egg

Florida

Cut &
Shoot

Cut Off

Doctor
Phillips

ost

Not to be outdone in the world of odd names, a villager from **Dull**, in the Scottish county of Perthshire, has proposed that **Boring** in Oregon be named sister town to Dull. (Just wondering ... why wasn't Dull, Ohio, chosen?)

By the way, it's thought that the word "dull" meant "meadow" in Gaelic.

Scotland

Dull

(And just for the record, Boring, Oregon, is named after its founder, William H Boring.)

Wales

England

Map drawn to the same scale as the United States.

Space stuff 1: how to greet an alien

Essential etiquette and survival tips for when that unexpected visitor to Earth arrives.

(Some things on this page are from the fictional side of science.)

1 If you have time, quickly change into something green. All aliens are green. (You know that.)

2 With your two eyes, look him/her/himmer in the eye.

3 Wave arms—in the welcome position, not the *yikes!* position. *Easily confused*

4 Offer a drink. (Oh wait, they don't have hands—forget this.)

5 Start a conversation. (You have to know the language for this step. Could be awkward.)

BUT *(and it's a big, hairy but ...)*

if he/she/heshe looks aggressive ...

6 Run away.

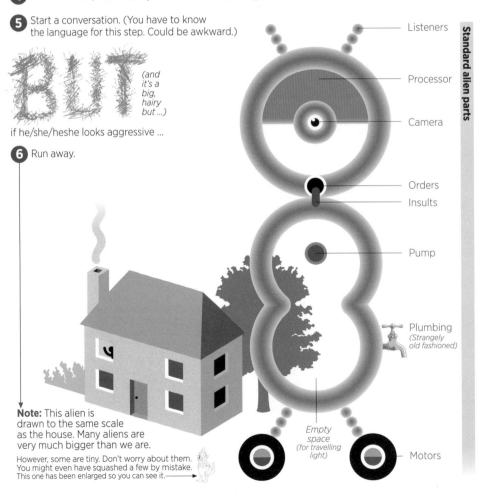

Note: This alien is drawn to the same scale as the house. Many aliens are very much bigger than we are.

However, some are tiny. Don't worry about them. You might even have squashed a few by mistake. This one has been enlarged so you can see it.—

Listeners

Processor

Camera

Orders

Insults

Pump

Plumbing
(Strangely old fashioned)

Empty space *(for travelling light)*

Motors

Space stuff 2: real tourism

Going to the moon? Don't laugh, commercial
space flights are coming sooner than you think.

It will be a few more years before you and I can go all the
way to the moon, but commercial flights into outer space
(which start just 100km, or 62 miles, up) can be booked
now. Trips for the first space tourists who sign up and pay
the full US$200,000 (more than 500 have so far done so),
are planned to start in 2013. They'll be launched from
Spaceport America, in southern New Mexico, aboard Virgin
Galactic's *Spaceship Two*. Each flight carries six passengers
and two pilots.

You can also book by putting down a US$20,000
deposit now and going onto a waiting list. (You
pay the rest when your turn comes and you get
the deposit back if you change your mind.)

At first, the trips will be short and suborbital (but you will
be weightless for part of the time). In the future, there will
be trips to the moon—taking about 9 hours—and much
later, to Jupiter (taking about 13 months).

And one day, astrotourists will be able to float in space
outside the rocket ship, just like the original astronauts.
For that, you'll need a real suit. By then, there will surely
be a terrific choice of colours:

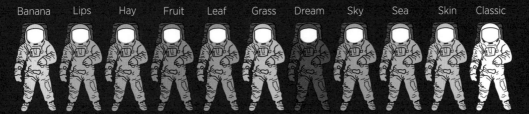

Banana   Lips   Hay   Fruit   Leaf   Grass   Dream   Sky   Sea   Skin   Classic

An emergency joke kit

Perhaps your flight has been cancelled and you are stuck at the airport for hours waiting for seats on another plane. You'll need a sense of humour. Try this.

① The characters

Pick three from this list

a plumber

a weightlifter

a lawyer

a scholar

a monkey

an ant

a grasshopper

an elephant

a magician

a psychiatrist

an alien

Miss Universe

God

② Their destination

Pick one

walk into ...

a bar

a bullfight

a gymnasium

a birthday party

a toyshop

a rock concert

a funeral parlour

a wedding

a kitchen

a museum

a muddy river

an ice-fishing hut

a xebec*

*Look it up!

What they say *(feel free to change the order of these in any way you like)*

the *[first character you picked]* says ...	the *[next character]* says ...	the *[last character]* says ...
hello	who's there?	it's only 4pm
who's here?	I'm thirsty	that'll be €100
I'm hungry	I can't see anyone	it's a small world
happy birthday!	that's stupid	eight times a day
knock, knock	I don't know	I'll have another
it's hot in here	nice legs	he's dead
12 porcupines sat down in a circle	I'm a vegetarian	just add water
my father was blind	it's just too big	I googled it
on Tuesday it'll be exactly 20 years	I'm cold	my dog ate it
how do you feel?	so what?	NUTS!
I've got sand in my toes	my antennae	that joke is older than I am
why are we here?	Van Gogh	whatever
	what's to eat?	#!*@&!?

How to play croquet

Six hundred years ago, in France, shepherds played *"paille-maille"*, a stick-and-ball game. *Paille-maille* (meaning "ball and mallet") became "pall-mall" when it arrived in England 200 years later during the reign of Charles II. Apparently the king was a fan.

Alternate roots
There's another story about the game's origin, which claims that it came to England from Ireland in 1850, where it was called "cookey". In England it became an organised sport, called "croquet", in 1868.

Anyone for tennis?
Croquet's heyday was short-lived. By the 1870s tennis was more popular, with the club at Wimbledon converting some of its croquet lawns into tennis courts. (It's still officially called the All England Lawn Tennis and Croquet Club.) It was an Olympic sport in 1900, but never again. However in 2005, scientists played croquet at the South Pole.

Croquet balls are made of ceramic, wood or cork-filled plastic. This is the actual size.

Croquet can be played by two people or two teams of two. (Part of the game's attraction in the 1860s was that both men and women could play.)

If four people are playing, one team takes the blue and black balls, the other the red and yellow.

If two people are playing, one person takes both the blue and black balls, the other the red and yellow.

The order of play is blue, red, black, yellow.

The ball weighs about 0.5kg (16oz).

Anyone for croquet?
Today there are some 170 clubs in England and Wales associated with the Croquet Association, and in the USA (where the hoops are called wickets*) there are roughly 200 croquet clubs, plus more attached to universities and colleges.

Variations
Extreme Croquet was thought up in the USA in 1920. It's played in the wild, over difficult terrain—in woods or lowland marshes—with heavy duty equipment. The first known extreme club was started in Sweden in 1975.
Gateball was invented in Japan in 1947. Today it's played there and in other parts of east and southeast Asia, and the Americas. It's fast and competitive.
Bicycle Croquet is played on bicycles. Duh.

*Did someone get cricket and croquet mixed up in America? The names of the games might sound a bit alike, but that's no excuse. A hoop is a hoop (balls go through them), but cricket's wicket is a very different thing. For a start, it consists of three wooden sticks (called stumps) with separate wooden "bails" balanced on top ...

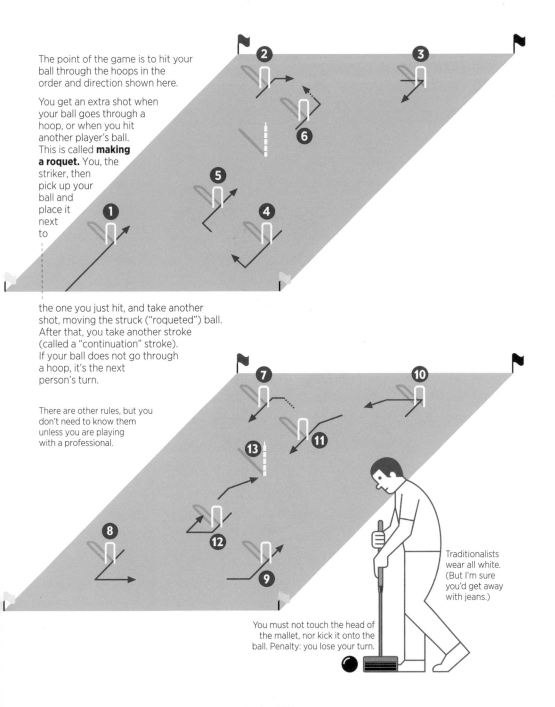

The point of the game is to hit your ball through the hoops in the order and direction shown here.

You get an extra shot when your ball goes through a hoop, or when you hit another player's ball. This is called **making a roquet.** You, the striker, then pick up your ball and place it next to

the one you just hit, and take another shot, moving the struck ("roqueted") ball. After that, you take another stroke (called a "continuation" stroke). If your ball does not go through a hoop, it's the next person's turn.

There are other rules, but you don't need to know them unless you are playing with a professional.

Traditionalists wear all white. (But I'm sure you'd get away with jeans.)

You must not touch the head of the mallet, nor kick it onto the ball. Penalty: you lose your turn.

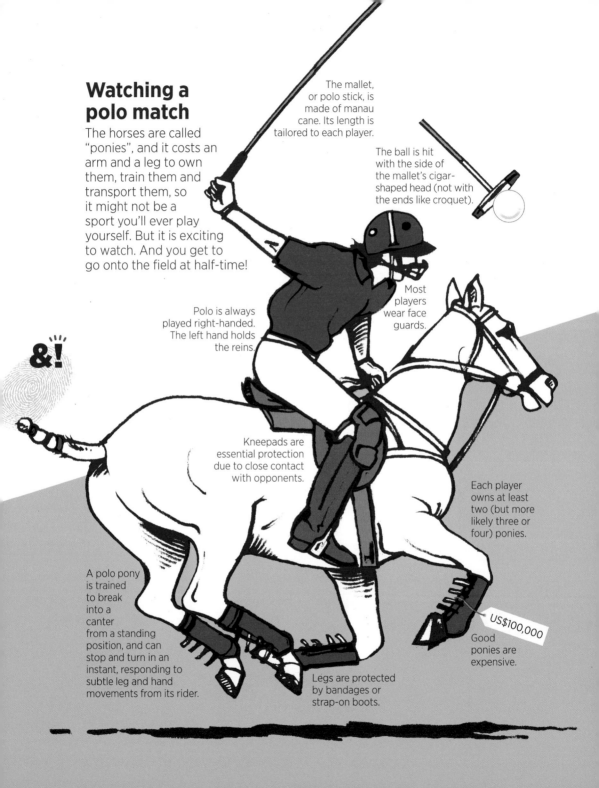

Watching a polo match

The horses are called "ponies", and it costs an arm and a leg to own them, train them and transport them, so it might not be a sport you'll ever play yourself. But it is exciting to watch. And you get to go onto the field at half-time!

The mallet, or polo stick, is made of manau cane. Its length is tailored to each player.

The ball is hit with the side of the mallet's cigar-shaped head (not with the ends like croquet).

Polo is always played right-handed. The left hand holds the reins.

Most players wear face guards.

&!

Kneepads are essential protection due to close contact with opponents.

Each player owns at least two (but more likely three or four) ponies.

A polo pony is trained to break into a canter from a standing position, and can stop and turn in an instant, responding to subtle leg and hand movements from its rider.

US$100,000

Good ponies are expensive.

Legs are protected by bandages or strap-on boots.

Rules

The simple point of the game is to hit the ball through the opponents' goalposts.

2

Usually there are six 7-minute **"chukkas".**

3

There's a 4-minute rest between each chukka. Players must change their horses. No horse can play more than two chukkas in a game.

4

At half-time, there's a 10-minute break, when spectators are invited onto the field for the tradition of **"divot stomping"** (replacing the turf the horses have messed up).

The most important rule is **the right of way, or line of the running ball.** This is the route that a ball takes as it rolls forward along the ground. The player who hits the ball (the black icon below) has this "right of way".

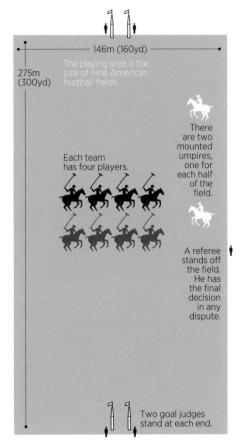

146m (160yd)

275m (300yd)

The playing area is the size of nine American football fields.

Each team has four players.

There are two mounted umpires, one for each half of the field.

A referee stands off the field. He has the final decision in any dispute.

Two goal judges stand at each end.

If an opponent (blue icon) can reach the ball without getting in the way of the hitter, he* assumes the right of way.

*Or "she". Polo is one of those sports where men and women compete equally.

A brief history

very!

● The modern game originated in **India** in the 1830s.

● British settlers took polo to **Argentina** in 1875, where it was enthusiastically embraced. By 1928, the official Argentine team was good enough to win the gold medal at the Paris Olympics.

● Today, the most important world-class polo tournaments are held in Argentina, but it's played in about 80 other countries.

Variations

● **Snow polo** is played on compacted snow or a frozen lake.

● Nonequine variants include: **bicycle, camel, canoe, elephant, golf cart, Segway and yak.**

● In East Africa, **moto-polo** is very popular. One person drives at speeds of 70km/h (44mph), while another sits behind holding a short mallet. One important rule: no sticking the mallet into an opponent's wheels.

Let's go by *fast* train

The world speed record of 574.8km/h (357.2mph) for a conventionally wheeled train was set by the French TGV (Train à Grande Vitesse) in 2007. First proposed in France in the 1960s, the TGV's first run, from Paris to Lyon, was in 1981.

In 1964, Japan's Bullet Train (Shinkansen) became the first high-speed train. This was followed by the Russian ER200 (also in 1964), and Britain's Intercity 125 in 1976. Belgium, Italy, Spain and Germany have built their own high-speed networks, linking with France's lines.

WHAT MAKES THE TGV SO SPEEDY?

The train was originally going to be powered by gas turbines, but after the gas crisis of 1973, plans changed to electricity carried in overhead cables and supplied by France's new nuclear power plants.

● **Connecting the pieces**
The wheels are attached to bogies that straddle two cars. This halves the number of wheels needed, saving weight. The cars are semipermanently attached to each other, making the whole "trainset" more rigid and improving aerodynamics.

● **High-speed power source**
Overhead electrical wires allow the trains themselves to be lighter.

● **Few ups and downs**
No incline on the track is more than 3.5%.

● **Gentler curves in the track**
A 5km (3 mile) turning radius is considered tight.

● **Light body**
It's made from aircraft-grade aluminium. This minimises the overall weight of the train.

Oo la la! Eet goes very fast!

Oui, and zey eet us on board!

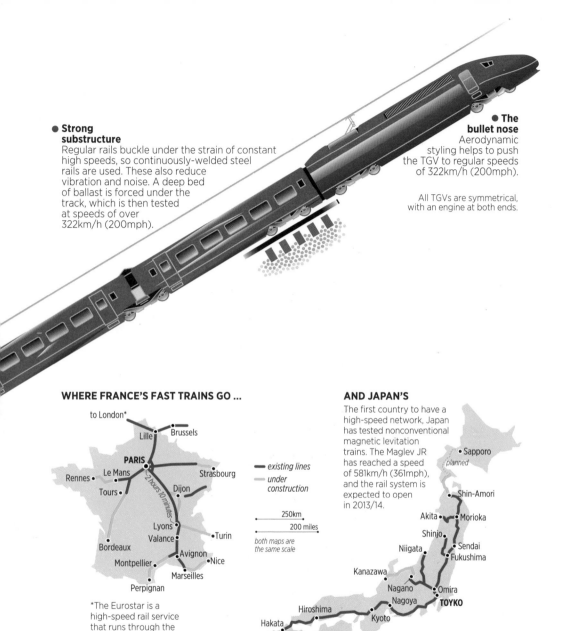

Strong substructure
Regular rails buckle under the strain of constant high speeds, so continuously-welded steel rails are used. These also reduce vibration and noise. A deep bed of ballast is forced under the track, which is then tested at speeds of over 322km/h (200mph).

The bullet nose
Aerodynamic styling helps to push the TGV to regular speeds of 322km/h (200mph).

All TGVs are symmetrical, with an engine at both ends.

WHERE FRANCE'S FAST TRAINS GO ...

to London*
Lille
Brussels
PARIS
Le Mans
Rennes
Strasbourg
Tours
Dijon
2 hours 10 minutes
Lyons
Valance
Turin
Bordeaux
Avignon
Nice
Montpellier
Marseilles
Perpignan

— existing lines
— under construction

250km
200 miles
both maps are the same scale

*The Eurostar is a high-speed rail service that runs through the Channel Tunnel to England. It carries 800 people in 20 cars that stretch to a total of a quarter of a mile, making it the longest passenger train in the world.

AND JAPAN'S

The first country to have a high-speed network, Japan has tested nonconventional magnetic levitation trains. The Maglev JR has reached a speed of 581km/h (361mph), and the rail system is expected to open in 2013/14.

Sapporo
planned
Shin-Amori
Akita
Morioka
Shinjo
Niigata
Sendai
Fukushima
Kanazawa
Nagano
Omira
Nagoya
TOYKO
Hiroshima
Kyoto
Hakata
Kumamoto
Kagoshima-Chuo

Tunnelling under the Thames

The London Tube is the oldest underground railway system in the world. It opened in 1863 (with steam engines). All the lines were north of the river Thames—getting trains under the river was a major problem.

But Anglo-French engineer Marc Brunel (joined later by his son Isambard Kingdom Brunel) was determined to do the job. Work started in 1825, but was delayed by floods and construction failures. In 1828, the tunnel was shut down completely for 7 years.

How Brunel built his tunnel

1 A wall of **wooden boards** was placed against the bare earth.

2 An **iron structure** protected workers from falling earth and rocks.

3 The structure was braced against the tunnel face with **jacks.**

4 The boards were taken down one at a time to reveal a **sliver of earth** that was excavated to a depth of 0.3m (1ft).

5 After excavation, the board was put back in place and the next one removed. When all the boards had been taken down once and the dirt behind them dug out, the whole structure was pushed forward 0.3m (1ft). Progress was slow: just 3m (9.8ft) of tunnel was dug in a week.

The total length of the London rail system is 402km (250 miles) and 45% is underground. It's the second largest ...

Taking a walk ...

Originally intended for horse-drawn vehicles, Brunel's tunnel opened for **pedestrians** in 1843. It was 0.4km (1,300ft) long, from Wapping, in the north, to Rotherhithe, south of the river. It became a steam railway tunnel in 1869.

through the tube

The tunnel was in continuous use until an overhaul in 1995 and then another in 2007. In 2010, the tunnel once more became part of **London's urban railway system.** The nickname **"tube",** now used for the entire system, originally referred to the deep circular tunnels carrying electric trains.

Showing the way

In 1933, **Harry Beck,** an electrical engineer working for the government-run Underground Railways, conceived a new map for the system. It was a radical change from previous maps; Beck used a layout based on the electrical circuit diagrams with colour-coded lines he was used to drawing.

Because of the difficulty of showing great distances between suburban stations and short distances between stations in the centre of London (which led to a very cluttered central area), it was clearer to **ignore above-ground topography** and make the distance between all stations uniform. This resulted in a "map" that was more a diagram than a conventional map.

Beck's classic diagram has been copied by virtually all subway, bus and railway systems around the world.

rail system in the world, after Shanghai's. London's deepest station is Hampstead, at 59m (192ft) below street level.

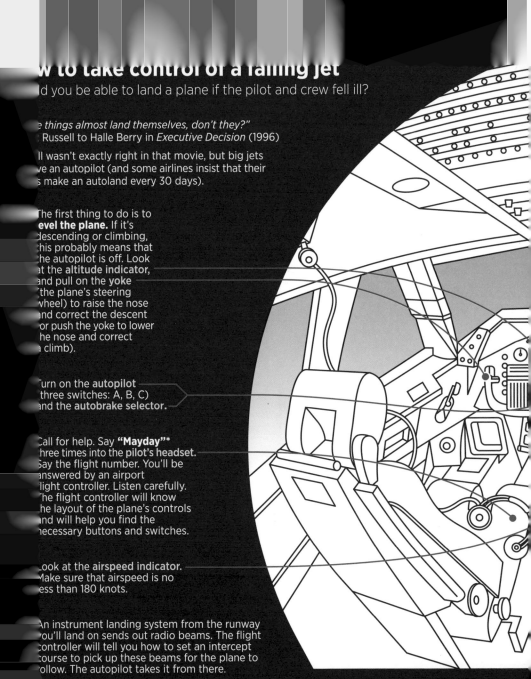

...w to take control of a falling jet

...ld you be able to land a plane if the pilot and crew fell ill?

...e things almost land themselves, don't they?"
... Russell to Halle Berry in *Executive Decision* (1996)

...ll wasn't exactly right in that movie, but big jets
...ve an autopilot (and some airlines insist that their
...s make an autoland every 30 days).

...he first thing to do is to
...evel the plane. If it's
...descending or climbing,
...this probably means that
...he autopilot is off. Look
...t the **altitude indicator,**
...and pull on the **yoke**
...(the plane's steering
...wheel) to raise the nose
...and correct the descent
...(or push the yoke to lower
...he nose and correct
...a climb).

...urn on the **autopilot**
...(three switches: A, B, C)
...nd the **autobrake selector.**

...all for help. Say **"Mayday"***
...hree times into the **pilot's headset.**
...Say the flight number. You'll be
...answered by an airport
...flight controller. Listen carefully.
...he flight controller will know
...he layout of the plane's controls
...nd will help you find the
...necessary buttons and switches.

...ook at the **airspeed indicator.**
...Make sure that airspeed is no
...ess than 180 knots.

...An instrument landing system from the runway
...you'll land on sends out radio beams. The flight
...controller will tell you how to set an intercept
...course to pick up these beams for the plane to
...follow. The autopilot takes it from there.

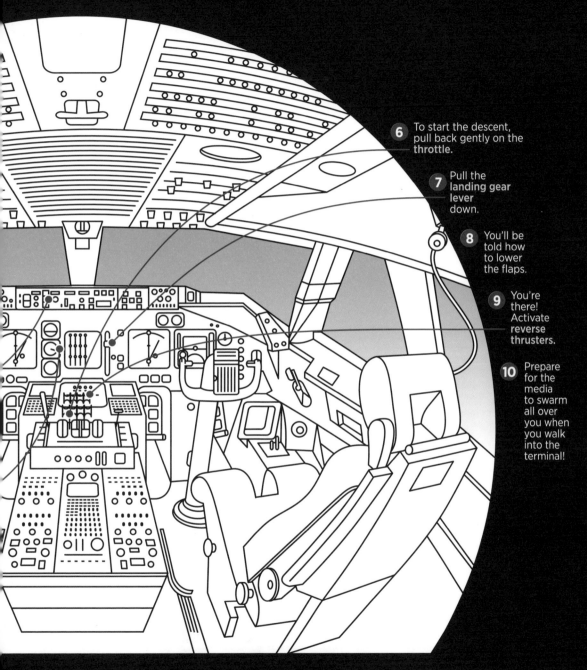

6 To start the descent, pull back gently on the **throttle.**

7 Pull the **landing gear lever** down.

8 You'll be told how to lower the flaps.

9 You're there! Activate **reverse thrusters.**

10 Prepare for the media to swarm all over you when you walk into the terminal!

Disclaimer: this is a simplified overview of the complicated landing procedure. Think hard before you volunteer!

Where are the world's highest buildings?

Empire State Building
New York City
381m (1,250ft)

When it was built in 1931, the Empire State Building became the tallest building in the world. It kept that position until the World Trade Centre Towers, also in New York City, were finished in 1972.

(443m or 1,454ft with mast.)

Willis Tower
Chicago
442m (1,451ft)

Formerly the Sears Tower, the Willis was completed in 1973, taking over the title of the world's tallest building from the World Trade Center Towers in New York City.

Trump International Tower
Chicago
423m (1,389ft)

Despite initial announcements that it would be the tallest building in the world, this hotel and office tower was scaled back after the 2001 attacks on New York. It was opened in 2008.

Eiffel Tower
Paris
324m (1,063ft)

The Eiffel Tower was built in 1889 as the entrance arch to the World's Fair. It remained the highest man-made structure in the world for 41 years, until the Chrysler Building was finished in 1930; that was eclipsed by the Empire State Building a year later.

Great Pyramid of Cheops
Giza
146m (479ft)

Built over a 20-year period around 2550 BC, this pyramid was the tallest man-made structure in the world for 3,800 years.

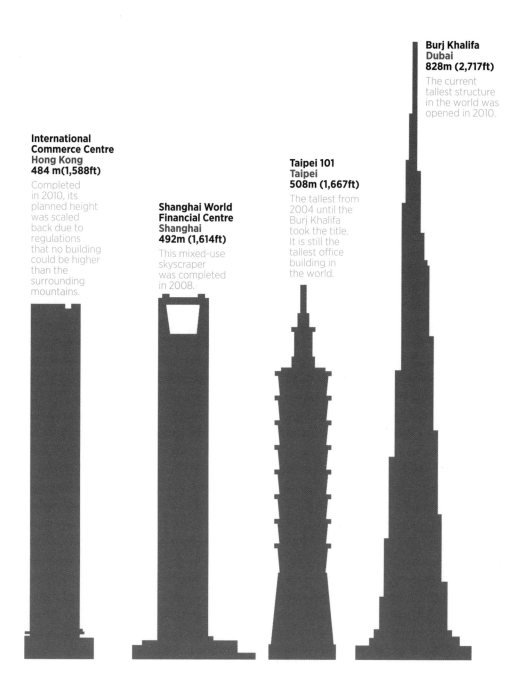

International Commerce Centre
Hong Kong
484 m (1,588ft)

Completed in 2010, its planned height was scaled back due to regulations that no building could be higher than the surrounding mountains.

Shanghai World Financial Centre
Shanghai
492m (1,614ft)

This mixed-use skyscraper was completed in 2008.

Taipei 101
Taipei
508m (1,667ft)

The tallest from 2004 until the Burj Khalifa took the title. It is still the tallest office building in the world.

Burj Khalifa
Dubai
828m (2,717ft)

The current tallest structure in the world was opened in 2010.

What's the capital of ...?

Study this and
win on quiz nights!
Or perhaps you'd like
to play quizmaster and
see how geographically
savvy your friends are.

The countries (states or territories)	Their capitals
Afghanistan	**Kabul**
Albania	**Tirana**
Algeria	**Algiers**
American Samoa	**Pago Pago**
Andorra	**Andorra la Vella**
Angola	**Luanda**
Anguilla	**The Valley**
Antigua & Barbuda	**Saint John's**
Argentina	**Buenos Aires**
Armenia	**Yerevan**
Aruba	**Oranjestad**
Australia	**Canberra**
Austria	**Vienna**
Azerbaijan	**Baku**
The Bahamas	**Nassau**
Bahrain	**Manama**
Bangladesh	**Dhaka**
Barbados	**Bridgetown**
Belarus	**Minsk**
Belgium	**Brussels**
Belize	**Belmopan**
Benin	**Porto-Novo**
Bermuda	**Hamilton**
Bhutan	**Thimphu**
Bolivia	**La Paz**

Bosnia & Herzegovina	**Sarajevo**
Botswana	**Gaborone**
Brazil	**Brasília**
Brunei	**Bandar Seri Begawan**
Bulgaria	**Sofia**
Burkina Faso	**Ouagadougou**
Myanmar (Burma)	**Naypyidaw**
Cambodia	**Phnom Penh**
Cameroon	**Yaoundé**
Canada	**Ottawa**
Cape Verde	**Praia**
Cayman Islands	**George Town**
Central African Rep.	**Bangui**
Chad	**N'Djamena**
Chile	**Santiago**
China (PRC)	**Beijing**
Christmas Island	**Flying Fish Cove**
Cocos Islands	**West Island**
Colombia	**Bogota**
Comoros	**Moroni**
Congo	**Brazzaville**
Congo (DRC)	**Kinshasa**
Cook Islands	**Avarua**
Costa Rica	**San José**
Côte d'Ivoire	**Yamoussoukro**
Croatia	**Zagreb**
Cuba	**Havana**
Cyprus	**Nicosia**
Czech Republic	**Prague**
Denmark	**Copenhagen**
Djibouti	**Djibouti**
Dominica	**Roseau**
Dominican Republic	**Santo Domingo**
East Timor	**Díli**
Ecuador	**Quito**
Egypt	**Cairo**
El Salvador	**San Salvador**
Equatorial Guinea	**Malabo**
Eritrea	**Asmara**
Estonia	**Talinn**
Ethiopia	**Addis Ababa**
Faroe Islands	**Tórshavn**

Fiji	**Suva**
Finland	**Helsinki**
France	**Paris**
French Guiana	**Cayenne**
French Polynesia	**Papeete**
Gabon	**Libreville**
The Gambia	**Banjul**
Georgia	**Tbilisi**
Germany	**Berlin**
Ghana	**Accra**
Gibraltar	**Gibraltar**
Greece	**Athens**
Greenland	**Nuuk**
Grenada	**St George's**
Guadeloupe	**Basse-Terre**
Guam	**Hagatña**
Guatemala	**Guatemala City**
Guernsey	**St Peter Port**
Guinea	**Conakry**
Guinea-Bissau	**Bissau**
Guyana	**Georgetown**
Haiti	**Port-au-Prince**
Honduras	**Tegucigalpa**
Hungary	**Budapest**
Iceland	**Reykjavík**
India	**New Delhi**
Indonesia	**Jakarta**
Iran	**Tehran**
Iraq	**Baghdad**
Ireland	**Dublin**
Isle of Man	**Douglas**
Israel	**Jerusalem**
Italy	**Rome**
Jamaica	**Kingston**
Japan	**Tokyo**
Jersey	**St Helier**
Jordan	**Amman**
Kazakhstan	**Astana**
Kenya	**Nairobi**
Kiribati	**Tarawa**
Korea (North)	**Pyongyang**
Korea (South)	**Seoul**

Kosovo	**Prishtiní**	Niue	**Alofi**	South Sudan	**Juba**
Kuwait	**Kuwait City**	Norfolk Island	**Kingston**	South Ossetia	**Tskhinval**
Kyrgyzstan	**Bishkek**	Northern Ireland	**Belfast**	Spain	**Madrid**
Laos	**Vientiane**	Northern Mariana Islands	**Saipan**	Sri Lanka	**Colombo**
Latvia	**Riga**	Norway	**Oslo**	Sudan	**Khartoum**
Lebanon	**Beirut**	Oman	**Muscat**	Suriname	**Paramaribo**
Lesotho	**Maseru**	Pakistan	**Islamabad**	Svalbard	**Longyearbyen**
Liberia	**Monrovia**	Palau	**Ngerulmud**	Swaziland	**Mbabane**
Libya	**Tripoli**	Palestine	**Ramallah and Gaza**	Sweden	**Stockholm**
Liechtenstein	**Vaduz**	Panama	**Panama City**	Switzerland	**Bern**
Lithuania	**Vilnius**	Papua New Guinea	**Port Moresby**	Syria	**Damascus**
Luxembourg	**Luxembourg**	Paraguay	**Asunción**	Taiwan	**Taipei**
Macedonia	**Skopje**	Peru	**Lima**	Tajikistan	**Dushanbe**
Madagascar	**Antananarivo**	Philippines	**Manila**	Tanzania	**Dodoma**
Malawi	**Lilongwe**	Pitcairn Islands	**Adamstown**	Thailand	**Bangkok**
Malaysia	**Kuala Lumpur**	Poland	**Warsaw**	Togo	**Lomé**
Maldives	**Malé**	Portugal	**Lisbon**	Tokelau	(None)
Mali	**Bamako**	Puerto Rico	**San Juan**	Tonga	**Nuku'alofa**
Malta	**Valletta**	Qatar	**Doha**	Trinidad & Tobago	**Port of Spain**
Marshall Islands	**Majuro**	Réunion	**Saint-Denis**	Tunisia	**Tunis**
Martinique	**Fort-de-France**	Romania	**Bucharest**	Turkey	**Ankara**
Mauritania	**Nouakchott**	Russia	**Moscow**	Turkish Rep. of N. Cyprus	**Nicosia**
Mauritius	**Port Louis**	Rwanda	**Kigali**	Turkmenistan	**Ashgabat**
Mayotte	**Mamoudzou**	St-Pierre and Miquelon	**Saint-Pierre**	Turks & Caicos Islands	**Cockburn Town**
Mexico	**Mexico City**	St Helena	**Jamestown**	Tuvalu	**Fongafale**
Fed. States of Micronesia	**Palikir**	St Kitts and Nevis	**Basseterre**	Uganda	**Kampala**
Moldova	**Chisinau**	St Lucia	**Castries**	Ukraine	**Kiev**
Monaco	**Monaco**	St Vincent & the Grenadines	**Kingstown**	UAE	**Abu Dhabi**
Mongolia	**Ulaanbaatar**	Samoa	**Apia**	UK	**London**
Montenegro	**Podgorica**	San Marino	**San Marino**	USA	**Washington, DC**
Montserrat	**Brades Estate**	São Tomé & Príncipe	**São Tomé**	Uruguay	**Montevideo**
Morocco	**Rabat**	Saudi Arabia	**Riyadh**	Uzbekistan	**Tashkent**
Mozambique	**Maputo**	Senegal	**Dakar**	Vanuatu	**Port Vila**
Namibia	**Windhoek**	Serbia	**Belgrade**	Vatican City	**Vatican City**
Nauru	**Yaren**	Seychelles	**Victoria**	Venezuela	**Caracas**
Nepal	**Kathmandu**	Sierra Leone	**Freetown**	Vietnam	**Hanoi**
Netherlands	**Amsterdam**	Singapore	**Singapore**	British Virgin Is.	**Road Town**
New Caledonia	**Nouméa**	Slovakia	**Bratislava**	US Virgin Islands	**Charlotte Amalie**
New Zealand	**Wellington**	Slovenia	**Ljubljana**	Wallis & Futuna	**Mata'Utu**
Nicaragua	**Managua**	Solomon Islands	**Honiara**	Yemen	**Sana'a**
Niger	**Niamey**	Somalia	**Mogadishu**	Zambia	**Lusaka**
Nigeria	**Abuja**	South Africa	**Pretoria** (administrative capital); **Cape Town** (legislative capital); **Bloemfontein** (judicial capital)	Zimbabwe	**Harare**

How to choose a diamond

Most diamonds, the transparent form of pure carbon, are 3 billion years old. They are the oldest things you'll ever own.

If you are planning to propose on a romantic holiday getaway, here is some information you might like to know about "a girl's best friend".

(1) Can it get scratches? No. The Mohs' scale (invented in 1812 to measure the hardness of minerals) shows that nothing will scratch a diamond.

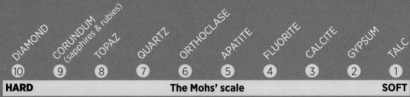

DIAMOND	CORUNDUM (sapphires & rubies)	TOPAZ	QUARTZ	ORTHOCLASE	APATITE	FLUORITE	CALCITE	GYPSUM	TALC
10	9	8	7	6	5	4	3	2	1

HARD   The Mohs' scale   **SOFT**

Each mineral will scratch everything below it on the scale, but not the ones above it.

&!

(2) What are the "4 Cs"? Experts consider these factors when rating a diamond:

CARAT
This is the weight of the stone.

CLARITY
This refers to inclusions (flaws) in the stone; the fewer the better.

COLOUR
This is the degree to which the stone is colourless. (You want as little colour as possible.)

CUT
The stone's angles and proportions.

(3)

So what's the difference between a **carat** and a **karat**?

Funny you should ask. It's all right here.

A **carat** is a unit of weight for precious gems. One carat = 200ml (0.007oz).

At that rate, your precious 5.4kg (12lb) cat is a 27,216-carat pet!

A **karat** is a unit of purity for gold. Pure gold is 24-karat, but it's too soft to make jewellery. So a ring that is 18-karat gold has six parts of some other metal mixed in.

What's the ideal cut? The form shown here, incorporating 58 facets, was developed in 1919 to maximise reflection of light from the interior of the diamond, making it appear to sparkle.

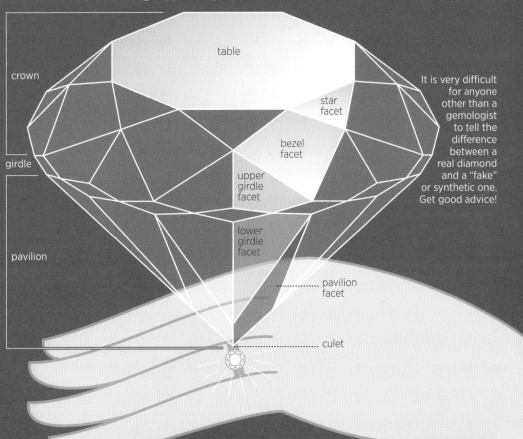

crown

table

star facet

bezel facet

upper girdle facet

girdle

lower girdle facet

pavilion

pavilion facet

culet

It is very difficult for anyone other than a gemologist to tell the difference between a real diamond and a "fake" or synthetic one. Get good advice!

The largest diamond ever found was the **3,106.7-carat Cullinan.** Discovered in South Africa in 1905, it was later cut into nine separate stones. One of those, Cullinan 1, or the **Great Star of Africa,** was the largest polished diamond in the world (530.2 carats) until the discovery of the Golden Jubilee Diamond (545.7 carats) in the same mine in 1985.

The Great Star of Africa is part of the Crown Jewels of the UK.

Running with the bulls

If you dare! It's part of the San Fermín Festival, an 8-day event starting on 7 July every year, in Pamplona, Spain.

The origin

The festival dates back to the 13th century and celebrates San Fermín, the patron saint of Pamplona. It's a mix of logistics and fun.

The logistical part is moving six fighting bulls every morning from their temporary corrals to the town's bullring for the evening's fights.

The fun part (if you can call it that) is running ahead of the bulls during their 825m (900yd) gallop through Pamplona's narrow streets. It is said that one year some daredevils decided to run in front of the charging herd, and from then on this very popular element was added to the festival.

The program

The order of activities is the same for all eight days:

8am The running of the bulls.

6.30pm Bullfighting with the bulls that ran in the morning.

24 hours Partying. The festival drink of choice is *Calimocho*. It's red wine and Coca-Cola mixed together in equal parts, with ice.

If you want to run

There are some **rules** (and the police enforce them):

● You must be **over 18.**

● You **cannot be drunk.**

● You must wear the **correct clothes** (see below).

Runners meet on the Cuesta de Santa Domingo. You need to be there by 7.30am.

A good idea: if you are new to the festival, don't run on the first day. Watch the run and see what you are in for.

Learn **the prayer** said by all before the run starts:
"A San Fermín pedimos, por ser nuestro patrón, nos guíe en el encierro dándamos su benedición."

The bulls
Six fighting bulls (and some lesser bullocks) run each day. The big bulls weigh about 700kg (1,545lb), which is a lot to be breathing down your neck.

white t-shirt

Official attire
red handkerchief*
tied round your neck

long red scarf*
tied round your waist

white trousers

*Can be easily and cheaply bought at the festival.

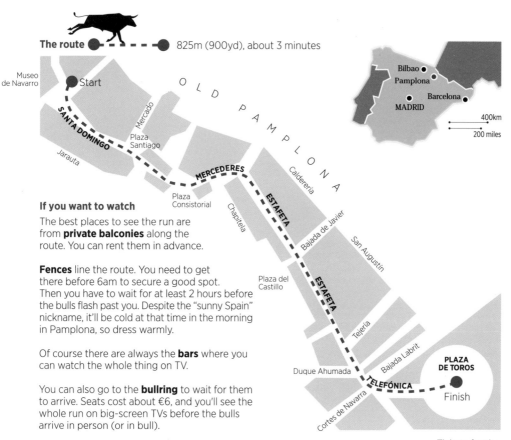

The route

825m (900yd), about 3 minutes

Museo de Navarro

Start

OLD PAMPLONA

SANTA DOMINGO

Jarauta

Mercado

Plaza Santiago

MERCEDERES

Calderería

Plaza Consistorial

Chapitela

ESTAFETA

Bajada de Javier

San Augustín

Plaza del Castillo

ESTAFETA

Tejería

Plaza de Castillo

Duque Ahumada

Bajada Labrit

PLAZA DE TOROS

TELEFÓNICA

Finish

Cortes de Navarra

Bilbao
Pamplona
Barcelona
MADRID

400km
200 miles

If you want to watch

The best places to see the run are from **private balconies** along the route. You can rent them in advance.

Fences line the route. You need to get there before 6am to secure a good spot. Then you have to wait for at least 2 hours before the bulls flash past you. Despite the "sunny Spain" nickname, it'll be cold at that time in the morning in Pamplona, so dress warmly.

Of course there are always the **bars** where you can watch the whole thing on TV.

You can also go to the **bullring** to wait for them to arrive. Seats cost about €6, and you'll see the whole run on big-screen TVs before the bulls arrive in person (or in bull).

It *is* dangerous

If you watch the run before you take part yourself, you'll realise that the biggest problem is people **tripping up in front of you,** not the bulls themselves. About 2,000 people run each day, and although the police try to stop anyone they suspect of being drunk, inevitably some runners have been up most of the night and may have bolstered their courage with a little something.

Since 1924, 15 people have died and 200 have been injured as a result of goring.

If you do fall, stay down, and cover your face. You'll have bruises. Someone will tell you when all the bulls have passed by and it's safe to get up.

Tickets for the **evening bullfights** sell out well in advance (the Plaza de Toros only seats 12,500), but you might be able to find a scalper who's offering tickets at not-too-inflated prices.

Riding a camel

One hump or two? If you are planning to view the pyramids on camelback, you'll most likely be on a **one-humped dromedary,** or Arabian camel.*

1

Camels are mean, they spit and they smell, but once you are up there you'll want to take pictures. Beware, because you're in for a **bumpy ride** and it's a long way down to the sand if you drop your camera, so make sure it's tethered to you.

2

Choose the right clothing

● A **hat** with a chinstrap and a flap at the back that covers your neck will keep the sun at bay.

● Put your **sunglasses** on.

● Roll your **sleeves** down, or slather your arms with sunscreen.

● Tie a **windbreaker** around your waist.

● Wear **baggy, long pants.** Tuck them into your socks. (Camel hair is scratchy.)

● Camels don't walk smoothly, so flip-flops will come off easily. **Wear boots or shoes.**

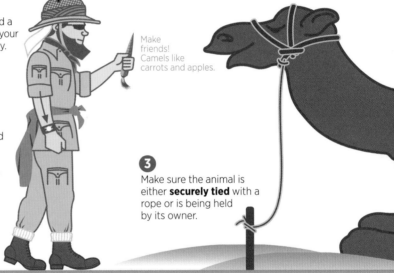

Make friends! Camels like carrots and apples.

3

Make sure the animal is either **securely tied** with a rope or is being held by its owner.

● Everything will get dirty and smelly, so **washable clothes that dry fast** are best.

● Be **respectful of local culture.** Women should not wear skimpy clothing. (Besides, the sun will punish you if you do!)

*The **two-humped Bactrian camel** is found wild in the steppes of Central Asia, where there are only about 1,000 left. There's a greater number of domesticated Bactrian camels living in Asia, but they are also on official endangered animals lists. You can ride them, snuggled between the humps.

4

Getting on
The "saddle" is a series of pads arranged around the hump, ending up as a flat platform. There might be either a stirrup or a small ledge attached to this to help you climb aboard. But if you are lucky, the camel guide will provide a **footstool, or small stepladder,** which makes mounting much easier.

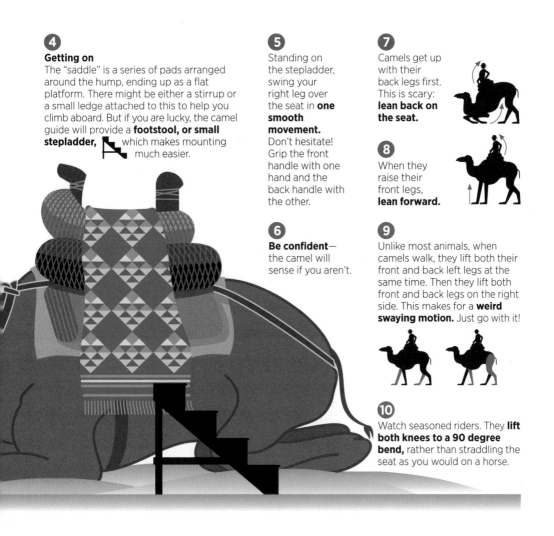

5

Standing on the stepladder, swing your right leg over the seat in **one smooth movement.** Don't hesitate! Grip the front handle with one hand and the back handle with the other.

6

Be confident— the camel will sense if you aren't.

7

Camels get up with their back legs first. This is scary: **lean back on the seat.**

8

When they raise their front legs, **lean forward.**

9

Unlike most animals, when camels walk, they lift both their front and back left legs at the same time. Then they lift both front and back legs on the right side. This makes for a **weird swaying motion.** Just go with it!

10

Watch seasoned riders. They **lift both knees to a 90 degree bend,** rather than straddling the seat as you would on a horse.

Thousand of camels were introduced into **Australia** in the 1800s. When motorised vehicles replaced the camels' transport role in the 20th century, many were released into the wild. There are now **more than a million** feral camels in Australia. Most are dromedaries, originally from India and North Africa, while a lesser number of Bactrians came from China and Mongolia.

Hey, Mum, Dad, why ...?

Knowing how to answer kids' questions will help pass the time on a long road trip.

Here, their questions are all about **colours**.

Why is the sky blue?

1 Thirty-two kilometres (20 miles) above the Earth, the sky is black.

2 "White" light from the sun is **all colours** of the rainbow.

3 About 29km (18 miles) up, the light meets **air molecules (◉).**

4 Light at the **violet** end is scattered more than the rest of the spectrum.

5 **This light** is scattered from one molecule to the next so violet light should dominate, then blue, etc.

6 But we see the sky as **blue** because our eyes are better at seeing blue than violet.

Why are clouds white?

1 Cloud droplets are much bigger than air molecules, so they scatter **all** the colours of sunlight.

This effectively makes the light appear **white** as the colours are scattered through the clouds.

Why is the sunset red?

1 At sunset (and sunrise), light from the sun is travelling **farther** through the atmosphere.

2 This means that more light at the blue end of the spectrum is scattered, leaving the **red, orange and yellow** for us to see.

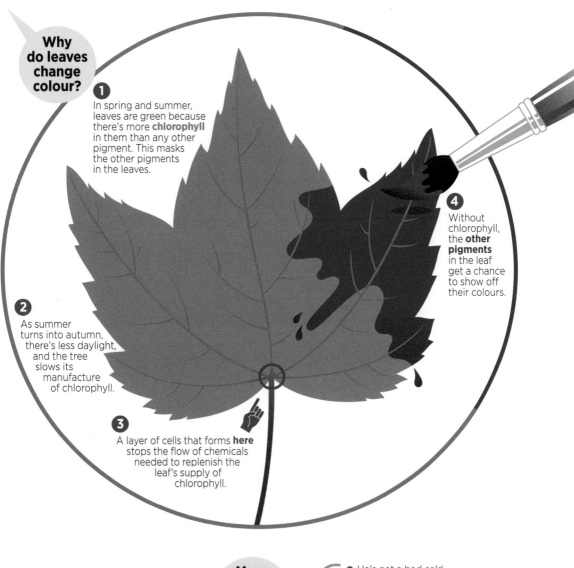

Why do leaves change colour?

1 In spring and summer, leaves are green because there's more **chlorophyll** in them than any other pigment. This masks the other pigments in the leaves.

4 Without chlorophyll, the **other pigments** in the leaf get a chance to show off their colours.

2 As summer turns into autumn, there's less daylight, and the tree slows its manufacture of chlorophyll.

3 A layer of cells that forms **here** stops the flow of chemicals needed to replenish the leaf's supply of chlorophyll.

Mum, why is Dad's nose red?

- He's got a bad cold.
- He's been out in the sun too long.
- You drew on it with my lipstick.
- He's been drinking again.
- He's a clown.

Sketching on holiday

It doesn't matter if you think you can't draw; just try it! The memories of your trips are so much better when you have painted them (or just scribbled something in pencil). Keep a visual diary. Years later, you'll wow yourself with stuff you had forgotten.

You don't need a lot of art materials. In fact, the fewer the better: if you give yourself too many choices, you'll never get going.

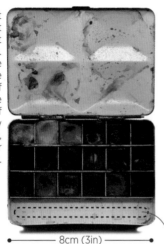

A flower in our hotel room. You can **use any kind of paper** that's around. (If it's cheap and thin like this, from a notebook made of recycled paper, the water might crinkle the page a bit, but who cares? The rock rose is preserved!

← 8cm (3in) →
This little **watercolour** box came with its own brush (in a travel tube that doubles as a handle). You just need a little water bottle, and off you go!

The view across the river from a friend's house.

Sometimes it's inconvenient to paint—a simple **pen or pencil** will do.

These seaside bathers
don't have to know
you are drawing them!

Drawing in nightclubs is a challenge; you can't really see what you are doing. But don't fret over any "wrong" lines you might make. As jazz pianist Thelonious Monk said when people criticised him for what sounded like mistakes in his playing, "there are no wrong notes in music". It's the same when you try to sketch a live performance: those wobbly attempts to capture a musician's intensity can add an in-the-moment reality to your drawing. This is François Moutin, becoming one with his 1805 bass in New York City.

These quick sketches of seagulls were done on newspaper. It's a terrific surface to draw on; don't leave it in the sun, though, it will go yellow surprisingly quickly.

Never mind;
accidents happen.

Details, details

Sure, you'll take lots of snapshots of your friends in front of the Eiffel Tower, or the Taj Mahal, the pyramids or the Sydney Opera House, but don't overlook the colourful, sometimes abstract snippets of fun under your feet, on walls or on your dinner plate.

And though many others have made this observation before, it's always amazing how often you see human faces in unexpected places.

The hammock smiles, the palm leaves wink.

No special effects, cropping or filters here. All the pictures were taken with a basic mobile phone camera.

Going batty

Bats account for about one-fifth of all mammals on Earth (and they are the only mammals that can fly). There are almost 1,000 species, and they can be found on every continent except Antarctica.

This is an insect-eating **Mexican free-tailed bat.** It's fairly small—this drawing is life-sized—but some fruit-eating bats have wingspans of 1.5m (5ft).

Some places to see bats

Free-tailed bats are found in southwestern USA, Mexico, Central America and northern parts of South America.

About 20,000 **rosetta fruit bats** live in **Buoyem Sacred Groves, in Ghana.**

The London Bat Group arranges evening walks in many **London parks,** where you can see **pipistrelles, noctules, serotines and Daubenton's.**

Spandau Citadel in Berlin is known to have been the haunt of **many species of bats** for centuries. The Citadel is a renaissance military fort built from 1559 to 1594.

Also in Germany, near **Bad Segeberg,** is the **Noctalis bat exhibition** and the nearby **Kalkberg bat cave,** where thousands of **Daubenton's** and **Natterer's** bats come to hibernate every winter.

About 90 species of bat have a **free tail** that extends beyond the flap of skin between their legs.

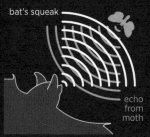
bat's squeak

echo from moth

Radar
When hunting for food, most bats send out a series of high-pitched squeaks, which bounce off any object in their path, producing an echo that's picked up by the bat's sensitive ears.

Ever since Bram Stoker included blood-drinking vampire bats in his *Dracula* novel, they've made regular creepy appearances in horror films and books.

Vampire bats are found in Mexico, Brazil, Chile and Argentina, but not Transylvania!

Vampire bats' entire food supply is blood. They need 2 tablespoons a day and if they go 2 nights without it, they starve to death.

Vampire bats don't suck blood from their prey, but they do bite. An anticoagulant in their saliva keeps the victim's blood flowing.

Draculin, a drug developed from this anticoagulant is being tested as a treatment for stroke patients.

Bat myths exposed!
(By talking bats, no less.)

> I hate the phrase "blind as a bat". Our eyesight is not bad at all. I mean, sometimes we don't even send out radar squeaks.

> I know! Very few bats contract rabies, and we die from it, we don't fly around! And we never bite humans, unless it's in self-defence.

The wings are a leathery, elastic membrane stretched over elongated forearms. Long finger bones support the tips of the wing membrane.

If the world were ruled by cats ...

They'd redesign national flags, so the rest of us would understand that they are in charge. (These new flags are not presented in alphabetical order, because cats don't care about things like that.)

The cat flag of
Sweden

The cat flag of
Japan

The cat flag of
India

The cat flag of
São Tomé and Principé

The cat flag of
Saudi Arabia

The cat flag of
South Korea

The cat flag of
Nepal

The cat flag of
Australia

The cat flag of
Italy

THE BOOK OF EVERYTHING

The cat flag of
Papua New Guinea

The cat flag of
China

The cat flag of
Senegal

The cat flag of
Brazil

The cat flag of
Canada

The cat flag of
USA

The cat flag of
Switzerland

The cat flag of
Sri Lanka

The cat flag of
Mauritania

INDEX

INDEX

INDEX

INDEX

INDEX

INDEX

SOURCES

WEBSITES

about.com; dotsub.com; electricaloutlet.org; paddling.net; wikipedia.org; wikihow.com; howstuffworks.com; desertmuseum.org; scientificamerican.com; fugufish.info; howany.com; icpri.com; sanfermin.com; squidoo.com; cio.com; yahoo.com; unhcr.org; wilderness-survival.net; howtoopenacoconut.com; polynesia.com; mosquitoworld.net; albanach.org; worldatlas.com; forbes.com; winearomawheel.com; mayoclinic.com; askmen.com; nih.gov; makemysushi.com; ehow.com; onthegotours.com; journeybeyondtravel.com; cnn.com; animaltourism.com; arachnophiliac.info; tramex.com; matadornetwork.com; survivalinternational.org

BOOKS

Rules of the Game, The Diagram Group • *The Worst-Case Scenario Survival Handbook*, Joshua Piven and David Borgenicht • *Jungle Survival*, UK Ministry of Defence • *Random House Encyclopaedia* • *The Riddle of the Rosetta Stone*, James Cross Giblin • USA Today Weather Book • *Rules of the Game*, The Diagram Group • AMA Encyclopaedia of Medicine • *The Human Body*, Charles Clayman (editor) • Northwoods Field Guides • *Mr. Beck's Underground Map*, Ken Garland • Edmund Scientific Star and Planet Locator • National Geographic Atlas of the World (9th edition) • *World Happiness Report*, John Helliwell, Richard Layard, Jeffrey Sachs (editors) • *Lonely Planet's Best Ever Travel Tips*, Tom Hall • *See Dad Cook*, Wayne Brachman • *Wordless Diagrams*, Nigel Holmes • *The Smallest-Ever Guide to Chocolate*, Nigel Holmes and Erin McKenna • *The Smallest-Ever Guide to Cocktails*, Nigel Holmes and Erin McKenna

ARTICLES IN THESE MAGAZINES

American History; Attaché; Backpacker; Business 2.0; Departures; eCompany Now; Field and Stream; GQ; Kid's Discover; Language Today; National Geographic; Navigator; Outdoor Explorer; Scholastic Scope; Sports Illustrated; Sports Illustrated for Women

FROM THE AUTHOR

Thank you to all the lovely people at Lonely Planet for making
this book happen; that's you, Ben Handicott, for continually, but enthusiastically,
assuring me that the work could be completed in a period of time that
was about same as the length of an ant's life (OK, that's a male ant; the females can live
up to a year, you didn't give me nearly that long!).

And you, Sophie Splatt, a friendly editor who allowed all sorts of
casual language behaviour, and who gently reeducated me in Australian/British grammar
and spelling usage. Along the way you offered terrific suggestions
that made the book a lot better. Mark Adams, you gave the book its
elegantly quirky cover and took care of all the little unsung graphic details
inside to make the book flow. Craig Scutt, you added the wonderfully funny index.
Project managers Errol Hunt and Robin Barton, you made great adjustments that
should stave off some of the inevitable 'you got this wrong' messages from readers,
as well as making sure the book finally got to the printer on time—just!

All you guys in Australia deserve medals for patience (not to mention
for living in a timezone so far removed from the east coast of the USA
that one of us might as well have been on the moon!). In Lonely Planet's London office,
my thanks to Publishing Director Piers Pickard for helping
to get the book going in the first place.

A few of the pieces first appeared in different iterations in magazines
and books. These are the art directors who invited me to work with them on those versions:
Mary K. Baumann and Will Hopkins, Paul Carstensen, Susan Casey,
Bob Ciano, Steve Hoffman, Holly Holliday, Susan Scandrett and Mitch Shostak.

As ever, my at-home editor, Erin McKenna looked at the spreads
and told me when she didn't understand something. I invariably baulked
at her comments, but later agreed that she was always right.

Thank you, sweet, smart Erin.

Nigel Holmes, 2012

ABOUT
—THE—
AUTHOR

Born in England, Nigel Holmes studied illustration
at the Royal College of Art in London and then freelanced for
magazines and newspapers for 12 years before going to
America in 1978 to work for Time Magazine.

He became graphics director and stayed there for 16 years.
Since 1994 he has run his own business, Explanation Graphics,
explaining all sorts of things for a variety of clients.
These have included American Express, the Smithsonian Institution
and United Healthcare.

He also creates graphics and illustrations for publications
such as the Atlantic, National Geographic and the New York Times.
He has written six books on aspects of information design.
His first children's book, *Pinhole and the Expedition to the Jungle,*
is now available for iPad.

With his son, Rowland, he makes short animated films
for clients that have included the TED Conference,
Fortune's Brainstorm Conference, Good Magazine and the
National Geographic Society.

THE LONELY PLANET
BOOK OF EVERYTHING

Publishing Director Piers Pickard
Publisher Ben Handicott
Project Managers Errol Hunt, Robin Barton
Cover & Additonal Design Mark Adams
Layout Designer Mazzy Prinsep
Editor Sophie Splatt
Print Production Larissa Frost
Thanks to Craig Scutt, Kirsten Rawlings, Catherine Naghten

October 2012
ISBN 978 1 74220 9630
Published by
Lonely Planet Publications Pty Ltd
ABN 36 005 607 983
90 Maribyrnong St, Footscray,
Victoria, 3011, Australia
www.lonelyplanet.com

Printed in China
10 9 8 7 6 5 4 3 2 1
© Lonely Planet 2012

Lonely Planet Offices
Australia Locked Bag 1,
Footscray, Victoria, 3011
Phone - 03 8379 8000
Email - talk2us@lonelyplanet.com.au

USA 150 Linden St, Oakland, CA 94607
Phone - 510 250 6400
Toll free - 800 275 8555
Email - info@lonelyplanet.com

United Kingdom Media Centre,
201 Wood Lane, London W12 7TQ
Phone - 020 8433 1333
Email - go@lonelyplanet.co.uk

Paper in this book is certified against the Forest Stewardship Council™ standards. FSC™ promotes environmentally responsible, socially beneficial and economically viable management of the world's forests.